TODAY,
NO KNOBS,
LETTING GO

I love you both so much.

Love, Lynn

Lynn Bryant

TRILOGY

Today, No Knobs, Letting Go

Trilogy Christian Publishers A Wholly Owned Subsidary of Trinity Broadcasting Network

2442 Michelle Drive Tustin, CA 92780

Trinity Broadcasting Network.

Cover design by Lynn Bryant

For information about special discounts for bulk purchases, please contact Trilogy Christian Publishing.

Trilogy Disclaimer: The views and content expressed in this book are those of the author and may not necessarily reflect the views and doctrine of Trilogy Christian Publishing or the Trinity Broadcasting Network.

Manufactured in the United States of America

10 9 8 7 6 5 4 3 2 1

Library of Congress Cataloging-in-Publication Data is available.

ISBN: 978-1-68556-949-5

E-ISBN: 978-1-68556-950-1

Table of Contents

Acknowledgements 1

Introduction 3

Chapter 1: The Painting 5

Chapter 2: Realization 7

Chapter 3: God's Instruction 9

Chapter 4: Today 13

Chapter 5: Recognize the Enemy 17

Chapter 6: No Knobs, Past/Yesterday..21

Chapter 7: Longing 25

Chapter 8: Regrets 29

Chapter 9: Decisions 33

Chapter 10: Grief 39

Chapter 11: No Knobs, Future/Tomorrow 45

Chapter 12: In Christ Jesus..51

Chapter 13: Letting Go 55

Chapter 14: Surrender..65

Chapter 15: Deception...75

Chapter 16: Cross in the Tiles..93

Chapter 17: Abiding in Christ..99

Chapter 18: Music Notes..103

Chapter 19: Gratitude 107

Chapter 20: Evening and Morning..109

Chapter 21: Pages of Days..119

Pages of Days Journal...123

More Pages Of Days 167

Acknowledgements

It is with deep gratitude to God for placing in my mind the illustration for me to paint, depicting biblical principles that visually helped me understand how to escape the bondage that I have been in for most of my life. Several years later, He inspired me to write this book to share the practical application of the principles that are represented in the painting in order to help other people to depend on Him and live with inner peace.

I appreciate the encouragement and suggestions that I have received from my friends, relatives, church family, and ladies' Bible study group. They are all very dear to me.

Thank you to my husband, who has been so supportive. He has even helped with household duties and cooking in order to free up time for me to write. Some days, I would find it difficult to find a stopping place as the words would pour through my mind.

Introduction

Several years ago, I received the image in my mind that appears on the cover of this book. As I painted it and meditated on each segment, the whole scene gave me guidance to begin the journey of recovery from the addiction of worry. Later, after painting the vision and practicing the scriptural principles illustrated in the painting, I knew it was God's will for me to share with others all that I had learned so that other people could also benefit. As I began to write, the words flowed through my mind, chapter after chapter.

I have attempted to express the enormity yet simplicity of the concepts of the Word portrayed in the painting, to bring freedom as the gift of each new day opens before you.

The last section of this book is a journal for you to record your thoughts, prayers, and personalized comments regarding each chapter and beyond.

Chapter 1
The Painting

The large hallway represents Today, which is where we live, moment by moment. The door marked with Past/Yesterday and the door marked Tomorrow/Future have no doorknobs because we cannot get into the past to change anything or tomorrow to control the future. We are to focus on Today.

Imagine yourself in the painting as I further explain the aspects of the illustration. The mail slot in the Past/Yesterday door is to deposit any negative thoughts of the past. Imagine that it functions like a shredder. The balloons in the container represent worry and anxiety. We are to take a balloon for each concern, walk outside at the end of the hall, and let it go with prayer.

We are not to waste our precious time today with worry and anxiety. As we release them and they float away to our heavenly Father in prayer, we cannot reach them to snatch them back.

When we release the balloons, we are also to give praise and thanksgiving, which the music notes represent. We can let go to God and have peace.

Look closely, and you will see a cross in the floor tiles. This reminds us of what Jesus has already accomplished for us and assures us that we can rest in God's sovereignty.

God is so good to show me pictures in my mind to better understand His Word. I painted it just as I saw it in my mind. I believe that He wants me to share what He has demonstrated so that you, also, can find hope for each day. In this book, I will explain how Scripture relates to each segment.

Chapter 2
Realization

It is my prayer that you can benefit from what the Lord has revealed to me through this painting.

I am now a recovering anxious worrier. I say recovering because it is a daily endeavor to practice what I have learned.

I had originally planned to give some background information to explain how I had come to the point of being addicted. Yes, I said addicted to worry and anxiety. But, on further thought, I realized that many of us have our reasons, predispositions, and circumstances that have led to bondage in some area of our lives. I believe that our great God wants us to focus on Him and His instructions on how to overcome the obstacles that would paralyze us and prevent us from living out His individual plans that He has for each one of us.

In order to move forward, we must seek the Lord to search us and show us what is holding us back and what is keeping us in bondage. In my case, through many years, God had shown me Scriptures, which are quoted in the next chapter. I just could not seem to grasp how to understand and apply them. I found some of my old notes and journals, written many years ago when I was struggling with these same Scriptures and subject matter of letting go and letting God. It was frustrating to me because I was consumed with feeling so responsible and compelled to oversee and fix everything and everybody in my family. I was very overprotective. I felt beaten down with guilt if I did not intervene. It affected my health. My body was in a constant state of anticipation of the next problem to solve.

Chapter 3
God's Instruction

Our Lord is so patient with us by taking us back to the same Scriptures. James 1:5 says that He gives us wisdom when we ask and without finding fault with us. Thank you, dear Lord. I had tried so long to figure things out on my own.

> Lean on, trust and be confident in the Lord with all your heart and mind, do not rely on your own insight or understanding. In all your ways, know, recognize, and acknowledge Him, and He will direct and make straight and plain your paths.
>
> Be not wise in your own eyes; reverently fear and worship the Lord, and turn [entirely] away from evil. It shall be health to your nerves and sinews, and marrow and moistening to your bones. (Proverbs 3:5–8 AMP)

The way for me to turn away from evil was by not expecting things to be done my way, in my timing, or according to my own understanding. Proverbs 8:13 includes pride and arrogance. So, all along, I did not see that it was prideful and arrogant to think that it was all on me to take on the responsibility of others in my family, that I could intervene and control the outcome. I was so overwhelmed with burdens that were not mine to carry.

Notice again Proverbs 3:8, which says, "It shall be health to your nerves and sinews and marrow and moistening to your bones." Think how obeying His instructions benefit us! Just think of all those years that could have been spent in better health, and my loved ones would be better off today. If I had let them reap the consequences of their own choices instead of rescuing and enabling them, even into adulthood, perhaps their life situations would be better. Now, I know that my "help" was a stumbling block on their way to maturity and self-reliance.

Okay, I know I can't take the blame for the choices they have made as adults. Besides that, I must give it all to God and drop it all through the slot in the door of the past.

James 5:16 tells us to "confess your sins to each other and pray for each other so that you may be healed." That is why it is necessary to be transparent before you, for my healing, and for yours. It was necessary for me to repent of usurping the role of the Holy Spirit by trying to handle everything in my own wisdom and understanding.

Many times, I have intervened in situations where I should have gotten out of the way and let go and let God. That is such a hard lesson for me to learn because I have always been a hyper-responsible, perfectionist type of person. The Lord finally had to put the messages in a painting for me to comprehend and apply with Scripture.

It takes practice every day to continue in recovery from this addiction. The dear Lord sends tests to check my progress. James 1:2–3 encourages us "to consider it pure joy, my brothers, whenever you face trials of many kinds, because you know that the testing of your faith develops perseverance." Our God is the awesome Father! He works with each one of us individually.

The following verses, Philippians 4:6–7, teach us exactly how to handle anxiety and worry. It is imperative that we take the time to study and apply every detail.

"Do not be anxious about anything, but in everything, by prayer and petition, with thanksgiving, present your requests to God. And the peace of God, which transcends all understanding, will guard your hearts and your minds in Christ Jesus."

What a Scripture; it sounds like a command.

Do not be anxious about anything. (You fill in your own concerns: _____.) Instead, what are we to do? Present our requests to God by prayer and petition (specific requests) and with thanksgiving.

To hold onto worry is not trusting our heavenly Father. Satan's trick is to make us feel guilty if we let go and give it to God. We feel compelled to take matters into our own hands with our limited perspective.

First comes the command, "Do not be anxious about anything." Our obedience must follow by responding in the manner that He gives us.

Present our request to God, "but in everything, by prayer and petition with thanksgiving." Relinquish it to Him. Relinquish is to give over control or possession.

Then comes the promise, "and the peace of God, which transcends all understanding, will guard your hearts and your minds in Christ Jesus." He will guard your emotions and thoughts.

Thank you, dear Lord, for the privilege to cast our cares on You. We can even release our loved ones into Your care. We can exchange our expectations for hope in You.

There is the poem "Broken Dreams" that I came across by Lauretta P. Burns:

As children bring their broken toys,
With tears for us to mend;
I brought my broken dreams to God,
Because He was my friend.
But then instead of leaving Him,
In peace to work alone;
I hung around and tried to help,
With ways that were my own.

At last, I snatched them back and cried,

"How could you be so slow?"

"My child," He said, "What could I do?

You never did let go!"

Before we delve into the various segments of the painting, let's pray: Thank You, Father, for Your patience with us. Please cause us to be receptive to Your transforming work in our minds and hearts. Give us knowledge and wisdom that transcends our own understanding. Cause us, Lord, to retain what You teach us and put it into practice. Your Word says in Philippians 2:13 that You "work in us to will and to act according to Your good pleasure."

We want to be obedient and be a pleasure to You. In Jesus' name. Amen.

Chapter 4
Today

The new day is a fresh beginning. Lamentations 3:22 and 23 tell us that God's "compassions never fail. They are new every morning; great is His faithfulness." It may take a little while for us to wake up and focus. But what a way to start the day! "This is the day that the LORD has made; let us rejoice and be glad in it" (Psalm 118:24). No matter what is going on or what is aching, the decision of how we start the day is ours to make. We can start the day with thanksgiving and praise or drag along with baggage, worry, and anxiety.

You do not have to carry the regrets of yesterday, the disappointments and hurts from the past or fear of the future into today. Those negative thoughts can pollute, rob, or paralyze you from the joys and blind you to the blessings of Today. Remember to run those negative thoughts through the slot in the Past/Yesterday door. Take those worry/anxiety balloons outside, at the end of the hall, and release them with prayer and thanksgiving.

Notice the music notes in the sky in the painting. Fill the air with songs of praise and worship. Fill your surroundings with thanksgiving. "Praise the LORD, O my soul; all my inmost being, praise His holy name" (Psalm 103:1).

God's promises are like a stack of beautifully wrapped gifts that have not yet been opened. They are for you and me. But we have not received some of them because we have not reached out to accept them. First, we must realize our need and acknowledge our heavenly Father as the Giver. We must be humble to receive and ask with the right motives.

It seems that we miss out on blessings that God wants to

give us for many reasons:

We can be so caught up with the things of this world and compromise that we miss His best for us. A very big hindrance is getting ahead of God instead of waiting for His direction. Another reason can be that we are harboring sin in our lives and hearts. Think about the Ten Commandments, which are our guide to identifying some of our sins that could be blocking our relationship with our God. Just because our society condones and encourages sinful living, it does not change God's commandments to us. He created us and knows what is best for us. He gave us His Scriptures and the Holy Spirit to teach us His ways. The Bible tells us to fear the Lord and serve Him with all faithfulness and to throw away our gods. "But if serving the LORD seems undesirable to you, then choose for yourselves this day whom you will serve. As for me and my house, we will serve the LORD" (Joshua 24:15).

There are so many things in our society that can become gods, idols, and addictions, such as personal power, money, entertainment, TV, social media, smartphones, video games, possessions, careers, another person, illegal drugs, worry, self-absorption, or anything that compromises, marginalizes or replaces our personal relationship with God Almighty. These things that distract our thoughts and actions sometimes go from a habit to an obsession, to an addiction, and then an idol. Time and devotion become centered on that god instead of the true God. His first commandment is "You shall have no other gods before me" (Exodus 20:3).

Spending time in His Word and prayer daily gives us the instructions that we need. "Search me, O God, and know my heart; test me and know my anxious thoughts. See if there is any offensive way in me, and lead me in the way everlasting" (Psalm 139:23–24).

In my case, the addiction was worry and anxiety, which substituted for trusting God and immediately going to Him when a situation arose. I was looking to myself for solutions, plans, and actions instead of consulting Him, and waiting, listening, and trusting Him. "Fear not, for I am with you; be not dismayed, for I am your God. I will strengthen you, yes, I will help you" (Isaiah 41:10 NKJV). "Never will I leave you; never will I forsake you" (Hebrews 13:5b). What wonderful promises! It is such a privilege to be invited to have a personal relationship with our Creator. The rewards are far beyond anything this world has to offer. The Bible is filled with His promises to us who have received Jesus as our Savior and Lord.

O Lord, please help me to walk in Your awesome promises. Please manifest Your promises in us as we yield to Your authority, sovereignty, and lordship. Help us, Lord, to get off the throne and allow You to take Your rightful place over our lives. You promise to give us peace and joy as we surrender all to You. You are God; I am not! I lift thanksgiving and praise to You. You are worthy, so worthy!

Thank you, dear Lord, for the gift of Today.

Chapter 5
Recognize the Enemy

Worry and anxiety are partners in destruction on the inside of us. They tear down peace, faith, and joy, plus cause physical and mental anguish. They replace the positives with the uneasiness of being out of control and fear of negative results.

A favorite trick of Satan is to tempt us to worry rather than trust God. But Scripture says in James 4:7, "Submit yourselves, then, to God. Resist the devil, and he will flee from you." Don't accept his nagging thoughts in your head. It is easy to obsess over past regrets and fears of the future, plus feel overwhelmed with the current life situation. Then, we find our Today is consumed with internalized pain and tension, which robs us of our peace and joy.

Each of us is concerned about many things, and rightly so. We should be concerned about ourselves as a person and our relationships with family, friends, co-workers, and even strangers.

We can be concerned about our relationship with God. The situations in our nation and the whole world, with the pandemic and political upheaval, are plenty to be concerned about. If we allow our minds to dwell on these to an excess, we become bogged down with worry. It then can bring in the companion to worry and anxiety, which is fear. It causes mental distress. We can become so depressed that we do not want to get out of bed. These anxious thoughts swirling around in a person's head are often from carrying a load that is not one that you, personally, are supposed to carry at all. It is sinking under the sense of responsibility and yielding to fear. We will never overcome worry until we begin to treat it as sin. It is! Worry is a lack of trust in our heavenly Father, who assures us in His Word of His love and care for us. "Cast your cares on the Lord and He will sustain you, He will never let the righteous fall" (Psalm 55:22). We must humble ourselves before God and repent of this sin. When we try to solve the issues by ourselves with our own understanding, instead of acknowledging Him and allowing Him to work things out His way or receive His guidance, it is exalting ourselves. I never meant to do that! He says to cast our cares on Him; like the yellow balloons, we must let go of them to our heavenly Father. We have a very limited perspective, but He sees all and is sovereign over all. Who are we, little tiny specks, to try to carry the load on our own shoulders? What pride to jump in to try to resolve all the issues that only He can. Perhaps He has a purpose for the trial we are experiencing for our own good, the good of others involved, or a part of His overall plan. The Bible instructs us, "Be still and know that I am God; I will be exalted among the nations, I will be exalted in the earth" (Psalm 46:10).

> Therefore, I tell you, do not worry about your life, what you will eat or drink; or about your body, what you will wear. Is not life more than food, and the body more than clothes? Look at the birds of the air; they do not sow or reap or store away in barns, and yet your heavenly Father feeds them. Are you not much more valuable than they? Who of you by worrying can add a single hour to his life?
>
> And why do you worry about clothes? See how the flowers of the field grow. They do not labor or spin. Yet I tell you that not even Solomon in all his splendor was dressed like one of these. If that is how God clothes the grass of the field, which is here today and tomorrow is thrown into the fire, will he not much more clothe you, O you of little faith? So do not worry, saying, 'What shall we eat?' or 'What shall we drink?' or 'What shall we wear?' For the pagans run after all these things, and your heavenly Father knows that you need them.

But seek first his kingdom and his righteousness, and all these things will be given to you as well. (Matthew 6:25–33)

His provision goes beyond our basic needs of food, water, and clothing. He provides for emotional and spiritual needs. For every kind of need that we have, He has the solution.

When we focus on the circumstances, our anxiety rises because we feel out of control. Worry robs us of that peace when we get our minds off God, with whom all things are possible. Every time we give in to worry, it is like telling God that we do not trust Him to take care of it. We, many times, think it should be done our own way and in our timing. Now! So, we attempt to solve it ourselves. We are getting in God's way. Worry is a sure way to tell that we have not turned the matter over to God. Even obsessing about something and trying to figure out a way to fix it in my mind is keeping me in an anxious mode. Repent and release those yellow balloons to our Lord!

Dear Lord, we confess this sin of worry. Grant us repentance, and please help us turn from this sin. We have been in that trap for so long. Cause us to immediately turn to You instead of ourselves when things arise that start our minds spinning and throw us into "fix it" mode. Help us to stop and acknowledge You, seek Your face, Your will, and Your guidance in the matter. Tell us when to speak or be silent. We love You, Lord, and want to please You in every way. Help us to rest in Your sovereignty.

Chapter 6
No Knobs, Past/Yesterday

Remember, the Past/Yesterday door does not have a doorknob. We cannot go through that door. The past is gone forever; we cannot go back to change anything. We must not allow the things that are now behind that door to interfere with today. Learn from the past, but leave it there.

Formerly, I thought it was expressing love for those people closest to me to help fix their problems and minimize the consequences of their actions or lack of action. But now I know it was enabling them to continue in their irresponsible and sometimes destructive ways. Taking on someone else's responsibilities that they are capable of or could learn to handle is not to their benefit. It facilitates them to stay in the realm of dependence. It is just hard to see someone you love suffer as a result of their own choices. When they won't or can't see that their life situation is of their own doing, it is especially hard because they blame the ones who have "helped" them all this time. Don't expect gratitude for all you have sacrificed. In fact, they may drop you when you explain to them that you now realize that you were wrong and that you were enabling. You had given the help in love, but it resulted in delaying their progress. I had always encouraged them to seek a relationship with God and turn to Him. Yet, instead of me trusting God to intervene in His way and His timing and allowing them to experience the consequences of their choices and decisions, I would step into the role of the Holy Spirit and attempt to remedy the current crisis myself. Oh, the audacity to usurp the role of the Holy Spirit!

Thank God that it is never too late to repent of that horrible sin and turn those loved ones over to our heavenly Father. I must remember to take all these sad regrets and guilt, put them in the slot of the Past/Yesterday door, and go forward with Today.

One time, I asked God to let me see behind the Past/Yesterday door. I wanted to see what happens to the past mistakes and sins after we have confessed them, asked for forgiveness, and repented, which means turned away from them. He did show me. It was totally black, as black as it is deep inside a cavern or cave. There was nothing to see! It was all gone! That is why there is no knob on that door. We only have Today. We cannot get into the past to make changes or correct our mistakes. Think about it. Even when an hour or a moment is past, we cannot get it back. That is why it is necessary to be mindful and prayerful in order to be in line with God's will all the time. Pray and listen for direction before action. Pray for His perspective. Be on guard; Satan will try to drag up the old guilt and torture us with sad memories of our wrongs. All that is really gone into the blackness behind the Past/Yesterday door. God tells us in Isaiah 43:25, "I, even I, am He who blots out your transgressions, for My own sake, and remembers your sins no more." Therefore, stuff those sad memories through the slot with confession and thanksgiving to our forgiving heavenly Father.

"When we confess our sins, he is faithful and just and will forgive us our sins and purify us from all unrighteousness" (1 John 1:9).

"Forgive us our debts, as we also have forgiven our debtors" (Matthew 6:12).

"For if you forgive men when they sin against you, your heavenly Father will also forgive you. But if you do not forgive men their sins, your Father will not forgive your sins" (Matthew 6:14–15).

Wow! That sounds very harsh. But think of what Jesus has done for us, taking our sins upon Himself. He took our punishment and took away our guilt. He suffered and died in our place. That is how much He loves us. How can we not forgive someone who has wronged us? But you say, "You don't know what that person did to me and how I suffered because of them and still do." Jesus took our sins and those of the whole world upon Himself.

"But God demonstrates his own love for us in this: While we were still sinners, Christ died for us" (Romans 5:8).

"You see, at just the right time, when we were still powerless, Christ died for the ungodly" (Romans 5:6).

"And when you stand praying, if you hold anything against anyone, forgive him so that your Father in heaven may forgive you your sins" (Mark 11:25).

We cannot imagine the agony it must have been for our heavenly Father to allow His only begotten Son to suffer and die as the sacrificial lamb in order to reconcile us to Himself.

Since God has forgiven us and reconciled us to Himself, we must, in obedience, forgive others. As you see, forgiving is not an option. God will help you if you ask Him.

"Then Peter came up to Him and said, 'Lord, how many times may my brother sin against me, and I forgive him and let it go? As many as up to seven times?' Jesus answered him, 'I tell you, not seven times, but seventy times seven'" (Matthew 18:21–22 AMP).

It seems that would mean, don't keep a count. We should always forgive. When we forgive and let go, it brings freedom to ourselves. We can pray for them and hope they will repent for Jesus' sake. I know it is easier said than done.

Some offenses are negatively life-changing. With God's help in processing the past, it is possible to forgive people and their offenses. After catching up on those, be ready to forgive for past hurtful memories, as more will occasionally pop up. Each time those memories surface, forgive and go straight to the slot in the Past/Yesterday door.

After meditating about the seventy times seven, it came to me that when Christ died for our sins, the crucifixion took place thousands of years before we were ever born. Yet, it covers us today. We know that Scripture says that Jesus is the same yesterday, today, and forever. He forgave us ahead of time before we ever committed a sin. He forgave in advance. We must do the same. Release the offender into God's hands. No need to be self-defensive. If we "fore give," we make a decision ahead of time to forgive before an offense occurs. When we have made that decision, as an offense does occur, we don't have to struggle with forgiving because we already have. Our Lord has poured out His grace on us, and He took our guilt upon Himself. We must not hold grudges. Stuff it in the slot on the Past/Yesterday door and "shred it." It is a step to freedom from stress for yourself.

Now let's look at the other side of the coin: "Therefore, if you are offering your gift at the altar and there remember that your brother has something against you, leave your gift there in front of the altar. First go and be reconciled to your brother; then come and offer your gift" (Matthew 5:23–24).

This time it is something you have done or said that offended someone else. Even if they just perceive it, then it is our place to go to them and try to reconcile. Ask God for wisdom, direction, and discernment in this matter.

Chapter 7

Longing

My great desire is for my grown children to walk with the Lord and honor Him with their lives. There is a longing in my heart for them to enjoy fellowship and relationship with Him and to be a delight to their heavenly Father. There is such heartache for parents of wandering children, no matter their age. Now, I finally realize that I am supposed to relinquish them to God and allow the Holy Spirit to work with them in His own way and His timing and His plans for them. All my efforts could not reach down deep within them where only Jesus can reach and apply His love to free them from their bondages.

All these years of intervening instead of trusting God to work out His overall plans for their lives is even more shameful for me because the Lord had given me personally a promise in the form of a poem.

This occurred many, many years ago, when my son was already out on his own and my daughter was not at home. My kids are eight years apart in age. I had been spending the whole evening in Scripture and prayer for my children. Later, I went to bed. However, the first lines of a poem came to me. I turned on the light, grabbed a pen, and began to write it down. As I wrote, more and more came to me. I will share it with you.

"Spring Forth"

Oh, seed of God's Word that is in them, my children,

"Spring forth!"

Don't let their outer lives deceive me into thinking

that the seed has died.

It is dormant.

Only God knows how and when that seed will begin to sprout.

They are aware of its presence. But they harden their hearts.

Have pity and compassion, Lord!

They are tormented in their emotional ills and sins.

Forgive them, Father, and heal.

Soften good soil; Your seed to grow.

Multiply an abundant harvest for Your glory.

Oh seed, you are battered and bruised in your dwelling.

But you are alive.

You will have your chance.

Be patient. You and I must, and wait with peace within.

Laugh and be happy, oh my soul.

Satan can set his snare, but the seed will remain.

The Word does not return void.

But accomplishes the purpose of God.

Great hope, little seed.

You wait not in vain.

The Lord will tell you,

"Spring forth!"

(Lynn Bryant)

It is difficult to hold on to faith and trust when we are filled with anxiety. I think of the apostle Peter when he climbed out of the boat to walk on water toward Jesus. "But when he saw the wind, he was afraid and, beginning to sink, cried out, 'Lord, save me!' Immediately, Jesus reached out his hand and caught him. 'You of little faith,' He said, 'why did you doubt?' And when they climbed into the boat, the wind died down. Then those who were in the boat worshiped Him, saying, 'Truly you are the Son of God'" (Matthew 14:30–33).

I think that is how we are. We look at the storm instead of keeping our eyes on Jesus and remembering who He is.

Forgive us, O Lord, and help us have unwavering faith.

Our God is almighty, full of love, patient, and kind. He promises to take care of us. He knows our deepest needs. Jesus took our sins upon Himself to reconcile us to the Father. While living on this earth, He suffered in every way as He identified with our humanity. He experienced heartache, sorrow, loneliness, rejection, and pain, physical, mental, and spiritual. Some of the suffering that He allows us to experience is to identify with Him. As it is written, "The Spirit himself testifies with our spirit that we are God's children. Now if we are children, then we are heirs—heirs of God and co-heirs with Christ, if indeed we share in his sufferings in order that we may also share in his glory" (Romans 8:16–17).

Listen to Jesus crying out, "O Jerusalem, Jerusalem, you who kill the prophets and stone those sent to you, how I have longed to gather your children together, as a hen gathers her chicks under her wings, but you were not willing" (Matthew 23:37). Do you hear the heartache like the heart of parents grieving for their loved ones who are not walking with Christ? God allows us to experience disappointment, betrayal, physical pain, emotional hurt, spiritual needs, etc. In this way, we are identifying with Christ's sufferings.

> Though now for a little while you may have had to suffer grief in all kinds of trials. These have come so that your faith—of greater worth than gold, which perishes even though refined by fire—may be proved genuine and may result in praise, glory, and honor when Jesus Christ is revealed. (1 Peter 1:6–7)

In support groups, identifying with each other's pain and validating their feelings and yours is a building block to repentance, forgiveness, and letting go. It is a stepping stone in recovery on the path to freedom. Jesus came to this earth and experienced our suffering. He identified with us. Then He took all our sins and agony upon Himself on the cross. The completeness of God's forgiveness is incredible. Psalm 103:12 states, "As far as the east is from the west, so far has He removed our transgressions from us."

Praise Your name forever! Help us to live a life of gratitude for Your forgiveness.

Chapter 8:

Regrets

We each have so many regrets tucked away in our minds. They are like cobwebs that clutter our Today. Oh, how we wish we could correct them all. There are the hurts we have caused others or misguided them. There are choices we have made that brought negative consequences for ourselves and others. It hurts just to think about those things. There may be times we had opportunities or nudges from the Lord to do a certain thing, but we did not.

There is nothing we can do to undo the mistakes of the past. You know where all those regrets of the past belong. We must stand in front of the door of the Past, ask God's forgiveness, forgive ourselves, run them through the slot and shred them. The more we clear our minds of these things, the more space we have to enjoy the freedom that the Lord wants us to have.

Think about the disciple, Peter; in Matthew 26:31, 33–34, Jesus told the disciples, "This very night you will all fall away on account of me."

Peter replied, "Even if all fall away on account of you, I never will."

"I tell you the truth," Jesus answered, "this very night, before the rooster crows, you will disown me three times."

Then, in Matthew 26:50, 56, the Bible states that Jesus was arrested and that all the disciples deserted Him and fled. That includes Peter.

In verses 69–74, Peter did deny Jesus three times. Immediately, a rooster crowed. Verse 75 states that Peter remembered what Jesus had said, "And he went outside and wept bitterly."

Talk about regret! Can you imagine that? But Jesus graciously restored Peter, and he went on to be a great apostle spreading the good news of the gospel.

The apostle Paul even persecuted Christians before he had the encounter with Jesus on the road to Damascus. At that time, he thought he was doing right. In chapter 9 of Acts, the account is given of his experience.

> Suddenly a light from heaven flashed around him. He fell to the ground and heard a voice say to him, "Saul, Saul, why do you persecute Me?"
>
> "Who are you, Lord?" Saul asked.
>
> "I am Jesus, whom you are persecuting," he replied. "Now get up and go into the city, and you will be told what you must do." (Acts 9:3–6)

Saul was blinded for three days until his sight was restored through a man named Ananias, whom God had told in a vision, "This man is my chosen instrument to carry my name before the Gentiles and their kings and before the people of Israel" (Acts 9:15). Saul's name was changed to Paul.

Can you imagine the guilt Paul must have felt when he realized that Jesus was indeed the Son of God and he had been persecuting His followers? After Paul knew he was forgiven, he stated in Philippians 3:13b, "But one thing I do: Forgetting what is behind and straining toward what is ahead." He let go of the past to go forward in his assignment to spread the gospel.

God does not want us to exist in the bondage of past regrets. Give Him your past so that He can take you forward in your purposes to bring honor to Him in all the endeavors He puts before you. God is so amazing. We cannot comprehend how much He loves us.

As Christians, we can look in the rearview mirror of our

lives and not see all our past sins since we have repented. But instead, we see the cross. Our sins are gone; we are free in Christ because we have been forgiven. It is important to learn from our personal history so that we don't repeat our sins. We must not dwell on the past but move forward in freedom from guilt.

Thank you, dear Lord, for forgiving our sins and taking away our guilt. We want to honor You in every area of our lives each day that You give us.

Chapter 9

Decisions

Decisions that we make on our own without asking and waiting on God's guidance and timing can affect us for our entire lives. One of our most important decisions is whether to stay single or get married. Our heavenly Father knows the plans He has for us. "For I know the plans I have for you," declares the LORD, "plans to prosper you and not to harm you, plans to give you hope and a future" (Jeremiah 29:11).

If we jump ahead of God instead of waiting for Him to select the mate for us, and in His timing, there can be major consequences. The consequences affect not only ourselves but our family, in-laws, children, grandchildren, etc. Even the children's genes are comprised of those of the spouse, as well as our own. It is vital to make sure the spouse is selected by your heavenly Father because He knows each person totally from His perspective, inside and out. We must trust our Lord above our timing, emotions, attraction, self-will, or any other motive.

After you have given it all to the Lord, then relax, and trust Him to orchestrate the beautiful story, whether it is for you to remain single or to marry in His timing and to whom.

When I graduated from high school, I was going steady with a nice guy. He asked me to marry him. I prayed and asked God to give me the answer. The next time I went out with him, he told me that his boss was going out on his wife that evening. Then, he said that it probably happens at least once in every marriage. That was my answer! I was not going to marry someone who had that mindset. Wow! How much plainer could God make it?

Four years later, I was so ready to be married and begin a life with a husband. I hoped it would be the next guy I met. I hate to admit it, but I had even told that to God! A short time later, I started dating a nice guy whom I met through my neighbor. As time passed, he asked me to marry him. He seemed to be the one. I don't recall asking God for confirmation.

Going ahead of my heavenly Father, I married three months later. Two years later, we had a baby boy. Eight years later, we adopted a baby girl. As years went by, I knew something had not been right in our marriage for a long time. Our marriage had become like a charade. I had lost trust and respect for my husband. We had two little children; what should I do? My parents divorced when I was a young teenager and my little sister was ten years younger. I did not want my children to experience all that a divorce would entail for them. The Bible says that God hates divorce. I never wanted to be divorced.

When we moved to another state, I learned about co-dependency. It was evident that my husband's nature was passive-dependent, and I was co-dependent. In a support group, I learned that I needed to stop taking responsibility that was not mine to carry. Even with both of us going to counseling and being involved in church all through the years, the marriage continued to deteriorate. By that time, our son was already out on his own and our daughter was to a point that it did not seem to matter to her if my husband and I stayed together or not. I could no longer live in the illusion of marriage. I felt so betrayed and alone.

The divorce was like a funeral for a deceased marriage.

What a huge mistake I had made by getting ahead of God. I have wondered what life would have been like if I had waited on the Lord's timing and direction. I am so grateful that God forgives and helps us learn from our errors, plus grow closer to Him as we go forward onto the path that He sets before us. Obey and trust Him is the way to move on.

A divorce recovery group helped me adjust to being single again. Later, I joined a Christian singles group at church. That was exactly what I needed. I learned some of the reasons that God hates divorce. The divorcee is exposed to loneliness, dating people even though seeing red flags, and temptation, to name a few reasons.

After being single for ten years, I decided that I did not want the emotional strain of dating anymore. I took it to the Lord. I prayed, "Lord, if you want me to be single the rest of my life, I will be fine with that. If it is Your will for me to marry, please guide me to the right person that You have for me, and make it totally clear to me that You want me to marry. In the meantime, I will be content just as I am."

About six months later, I had changed jobs. On my lunch break, I ran into a young lady with whom I had formerly worked at my old job, so we sat together to have our lunch. Another young lady friend of hers came to join us. I had not met her before.

The next evening, I received a phone call from a man who said he was the other young lady's dad and that the two ladies had told him that they thought we should meet. I "interviewed" him on the phone, then agreed to go out to dinner that weekend. We hit it off right away. He was a great guy, with no red flags. As months went by, I realized that I loved him. It was a comfortable, natural feeling to be with him. One evening he asked me to marry him. It was so strange. When he asked me, I heard the words come out of my mouth, "I want to marry you." It just came right out of my mouth before I could even think about it. It surprised me. It was like someone else had spoken those words from my mouth. I believed that to be my heavenly Father's answer to my prayer.

We were married and were very happy for eight years and four months. Then, he suddenly had a heart attack and died. I was absolutely devastated.

Sometime later, I wrote down my thoughts.

"Through the Valley"

God gave me numbness to make me able to bear the pain,
to grieve and come to grips with what had happened.
Sometimes, I had a flood of tears, and sometimes, I could not cry.
I was grateful to know the one I loved was in heaven with our Lord.
I needed time to rest since my thinking was so
scrambled and confused.
I prayed for the dear Lord to help me receive His comfort and love
to heal my broken heart and the strength
to put one foot in front of the other, moment by moment.
Eventually, the fog began to lift from
this valley of the shadow of death;
I was able to have joy in the happy memories.
(Lynn Bryant)

It was a big adjustment to live alone again. Yet, I knew the Lord was with me. He even gave me these Scriptures, Psalm 4:8, "I will lie down and sleep in peace, for you alone, O LORD, make me dwell in safety," and Isaiah 54:5, "For your Maker is your husband—the LORD Almighty is His name—the Holy One of Israel is your Redeemer."

My mother had been having health problems, including memory loss and confusion. It was apparent that she needed me to be near to assist her. I was able to move her into the house on the next street just behind my house. That was a blessing for both of us.

I was content to be single and devote myself to my mother's care.

For several years, I had been attending a group on Wednesdays at church. We would sing praise songs and hymns. Then, the pastor or one of the staff members would have a short Bible lesson. It was always a midweek boost for me.

A man started attending with an older gentleman in our group. As time went on, if the older gentleman was absent, the other guy came by himself. They always sat in the two seats by the door. One Wednesday, I arrived late because of taking care of my mother. The first seat by the door was vacant, so I quietly sat down there.

When the meeting ended, that man sitting next to me introduced himself. He asked me, "How long has it been since your husband passed away?" I responded, "Two years." He told me that it had been nine years since his wife died. I think it was a week or two later that He asked me out to lunch. I asked him to let me think about it. I hesitated because I had not gone out since my late husband's death. I prayed and talked to my pastor and some close friends. The next Wednesday, I told him that if he still wanted to go out, I would like to go to lunch with him. He later told me that when I hesitated, he thought I was just giving him the brush off. After months of dating, he said he knew I had told him that I had no intention of marrying again but that his feelings were that he would like for us to marry. However, he said he would not say anything else about it, but if I changed my mind, just let him know. Well, the next year, after much praying, seeking God's direction and His will, the Lord told me, "Don't be afraid to receive the gift of him as your husband." That was clear to me! We are so blessed to have each other.

These are major decisions, but even things that seem small can make a big difference. Whatever the decision you need to make, be sure to pray, ask God for His direction, and wait for His answer and timing.

"Wait for the LORD, be strong and take heart and wait for the LORD" (Psalm 27:14).

Chapter 10

Grief

My mother struggled with physical pain for many years and dementia for about five years. It was a labor of love to take care of her, but so hard to see her suffer even with all the medical help. Eventually, her doctor and my doctor told me that it was time to move her into assisted living. I was physically and emotionally drained. She protested at first but then adjusted to her new surroundings. I checked on her and visited with her almost daily. Sometimes she would hallucinate. One time, she had it in her mind that I had been in an accident, and the doctors had to cut my legs off. She was fighting the staff, trying to come to me. She even bit a nurse. They called me to hurry over to calm her down. I showed her that I was all right and had my legs. It was determined that she had a roaring urinary tract infection. She had hallucinated before with a urinary tract infection. As the dementia accelerated, distorting her thinking, and her physical problems required more care, she had to be moved to a memory care facility. Bless her heart. She told me that all the other people there looked normal, but they were not. We had discussed dementia from the time she had been diagnosed. So, I would explain to her again about dementia. We had to laugh at the funny things she would say and do. When I arrived one day, the attendant told me that Mother had been under her bed. They asked her what she was doing under there. She said, "Looking for Lynn and Jesus." Oh, how I miss her. We were very close, best friends, and always there for each other.

She fell, trying to get out of bed on her own. She was sent to the hospital for thirteen days with five broken ribs. Then on to a nursing home. It was hard for her. While she could still talk, she said that she did not know anyone there. She was age ninety-one and so confused. My mother was failing quickly. The year before, she had begun saying that she was ready to go home to Jesus. I knew the time was short. She had stopped eating, drinking, and talking. I told her that it was okay to let go; she had suffered so long.

I was with her when she took her last breath. My beautiful Mother.

"Good Bye"

The time came. The struggles are gone.
All the confusion is now in the past.
Dear, sweet soul is home at last.
Relief and sorrow mixed as one.
The fog is thick; the numbness abides
to make us able to bear emotions tide.
Thank You, Lord, that we can find
rest in Your comfort and joy in Your strength.
Blessed be the name of the Lord.
(Lynn Bryant)

Three years later, I lost my sister, too. She suddenly became very ill and survived only a week in the ICU. She had many medical problems. As my baby sister by ten years, she referred to me affectionately as her other mother. It is still hard to believe that she is gone.

My brother had died when he was sixty. My father had died when he was almost seventy. I am the only one left of my original family. It is a strange feeling.

The Holy Spirit is the Comforter. He has given me strength

to carry on. He has blessed me as my life goes forward daily on the path He has set before me.

It takes time to heal, so rest in Him as He walks with you day by day, step by step. Scripture tells us, "Blessed are the dead who die in the Lord from now on." "Yes," says the Spirit, "they will rest from their labor, for their deeds will follow them" (Revelation 14:13).

Whether it is the death of a loved one or the death of a marriage, it is unfulfilled expectations. It makes me think of a puzzle with missing pieces and some broken pieces. The picture on the box is faded and partly torn off. It does not matter how many times we try to put it together; it cannot be completed. No matter how much your mind dwells on trying to rearrange the ragged pieces, it is not going to happen. We must surrender the puzzle to our heavenly Father and let go. Our God has plans and purposes for you. Life goes on for those still living on this earth. Life goes on for those who have finished their time on earth and have gone on to be with the Lord. Rejoice and be glad; there will one day be a great reunion!

It is all right for us to bring our sorrow and grief to Father God. Come with gratitude for the time we had with our dear ones and for the wonderful memories. Rejoice as they continue their walk with Jesus in the heavenly realm. Our loved ones would want us to continue our journey with the Holy Spirit here on earth. God still has His purposes for you to go on living. The Lord has promised to never leave you or forsake you. Sometimes He carries us until we regain strength and courage to come out into the light again. Our loving Father gives us rest as we lean on Him, and He will see us through. Go outside and release that beautiful balloon into His care. To release is not to abandon but to trust. Let the Lord wrap His arms around you and receive His love. Bright tomorrows will come as you are being prepared for what He has planned for you. Glory be to God Almighty forever.

When the end was drawing near for my mother to leave this earth, the Lord showed me another painting in my mind. This one was of a sparrow on a nest looking toward a bright light in the sky. I thought of the words of a song, "I'll fly away, oh glory." Mother knew in her spirit the time was near. She wanted that time to hurry up. So, we began to pray for a gentle passing for her.

When my late husband died, I grasped a better understanding of Psalm 23:

> The LORD is my shepherd; I shall not want.
>
> He makes me to lie down in green pastures;
>
> He leads me beside still waters.
>
> He restores my soul;
>
> He leads me in paths of righteousness
>
> For His name's sake.
>
> Yea, though I walk through the valley of
>
> the shadow of death,
>
> I will fear no evil;
>
> For You are with me;
>
> Your rod and Your staff, they comfort me.
>
> You prepare a table before me in the
>
> presence of my enemies;
>
> You anoint my head with oil;
>
> My cup runs over.
>
> Surely goodness and mercy shall follow me
>
> All the days of my life;
>
> And I will dwell in the house of the LORD
>
> Forever.
>
> (Psalm 23 NKJV)

When Jesus was born, the shepherds were very low on the social scale. Yet, Jesus humbled Himself, came to earth, and became our Shepherd. He guides us, supplies all our needs, quiets, and restores our souls. It is amazing that, for His name's sake, we are led on the paths of righteousness. As children of God, we want to honor His name by walking in those paths and reflect who He is. Even though we must pass through the valley of the shadow of death, we don't have to fear because the Son of God has defeated death which is now a transition to life for eternity for those who have received Jesus as their Lord and Savior. When a loved one leaves this earth, and we are the ones who remain, we experience that shadow too. However, we have the wonderful assurance that they are with Christ. The Holy Spirit comforts us in our grief. God gives us goodness and mercy in all our lives. Our Redeemer has prepared a place for each one of us to dwell with Him forever.

It is so wonderful that God offers this eternal life to everyone. Scripture proclaims, "Brothers, we do not want you to be ignorant about those who fall asleep [die], or to grieve like the rest of men, who have no hope. We believe that Jesus died and rose again and so we believe that God will bring with Jesus those who have fallen asleep in him" (1 Thessalonians 4:13–14).

One of my neighbors was so angry at God for letting her father die. Only God knows what would have been in the future for the deceased loved one if he had lived. For those who die in Christ, in His grace, He may have spared them from things worse than death. We can have peace knowing they are with the Lord.

We grieve for ourselves, thinking of all the wonderful times that we are missing because our loved one is not with us here anymore. Also, thinking of what they are missing here. Remember that they are experiencing wonders that are so far superior to anything on this earth. Pray that God will give you the grace, comfort, and strength to release your beloved into a love that is greater than we can imagine.

Your devotion to your loved one and the precious memories are yours to keep. Think about the joy you had holding them for a while. Let the Lord embrace you. Give Him your hand to lead you on, step by step, and one day, hour, or moment at a time.

When those we love are grieving, let them know you are there for them but don't try to talk them out of their grief. The Lord is walking with them through this valley of the shadow of death in a way that is suited to them. Healing is a process. You can do kind things for them, but give them space. Let them cry.

Chapter 11
No Knobs, Future/Tomorrow

As you stand before the door marked Future/Tomorrow, what runs through your mind? Is it excitement and anticipation or perhaps dread and fear?

Sometimes it depends on what season of life we are in at the time. Especially when we are young, there are so many dreams and aspirations ahead, many adventures, and plans. Some children, however, who are in an abusive situation, live in fear and dread. This is true for abused spouses as well as other people who are in bondage under someone else's harsh control. It can be physical, mental, emotional, and even spiritual. It does not have to be in an abusive situation. It can be in the chains of addiction or chronic health problems. It can even be such an enormous disappointment that it is hard to bear, hard to go on to face tomorrow.

As a parent, we have hopes and dreams for our children. We look forward to the customary milestones in their lives. In marriage, we have expectations of our spouse and of our lives together.

For some of us, dreams are fulfilled. For some, they have been shattered. It can affect our view of the future. I would dare to say that we all have had a mixture of both. We live and grow, experiencing good times and bad times.

It makes me think about Joseph, the son of Jacob, who had a prophetic dream. You can read all about it in Genesis 37:5–36. The brothers already knew that their father loved Joseph the most and even made a special richly ornamented coat for him. His brothers already hated Joseph. It made his brothers furious when he told them about his dream because it meant that

Joseph would eventually reign over them. Then he had another dream that meant that their father and mother would bow down to him as well as all his eleven brothers. Long story short, the brothers wanted to kill him, but their brother, Reuben, told them to leave Joseph there in the desert inside a cistern that had no water in it. A caravan came through on their way to Egypt. The brothers decided to sell Joseph to them as a slave. They killed an animal and put the blood on Joseph's coat, then took it to their father and lied that a wild animal had killed him.

You can go to Genesis chapters 39–50 to read the rest of the story of all that Joseph experienced in Egypt, going from a slave to prison time and from interpreting Pharaoh's dreams to being in command of Egypt just under Pharaoh. It is an incredible adventure. In Genesis 39:23, it states that the LORD was with Joseph and gave him success in whatever he did. Many years later, he was reconciled with his brothers. He told them, "You intended to harm me, but God intended it for good to accomplish what is now being done, the saving of many lives" (Genesis 50:20).

Throughout Scripture, there are many passages that exemplify God's sovereignty.

"And we know that in all things God works for the good of those who love him, who have been called according to his purpose" (Romans 8:28).

"Consider it pure joy, my brothers, whenever you face trials of many kinds, because you know that the testing of your faith develops perseverance" (James 1:2–3).

There is a time for everything and a season for every activity under heaven:

> A time to be born and a time to die, a time to plant and a time to uproot, a time to kill and a time to heal, a time to

tear down and a time to build, a time to weep and a time to laugh, a time to mourn and a time to dance, a time to scatter stones and a time to gather them, a time to embrace and a time to refrain, a time to search and a time to give up, a time to keep and a time to throw away, a time to tear and a time to mend, a time to be silent and a time to speak, a time to love and a time to hate, a time for war and a time for peace. (Ecclesiastes 3:1–8)

A time to hate? Yes, but not the hate that Joseph's brothers had toward him. Examples are in Proverbs 13:5, "The righteous hate what is false," and in Psalm 97:10, "Let those who love the LORD hate evil." In Proverbs 6:16–19, there are things listed that the LORD hates: "haughty eyes, a lying tongue, hands that shed innocent blood, a heart that devises wicked schemes, feet that are quick to rush into evil, a false witness who pours out lies, and a man who stirs up dissension among brothers."

The Bible assures us that we don't have to dread what is ahead in the future. Great is our God's faithfulness, and His mercies are new every morning. "The LORD is good to those whose hope is in him, to the one who seeks him" (Lamentations 3:25).

He knows what is ahead in your life, and He promises never to leave you or forsake you.

"But seek first his kingdom and his righteousness, and all these things will be given to you as well. Therefore, do not worry about tomorrow, for tomorrow will worry about itself. Each day has enough trouble of its own" (Matthew 6:34).

Now listen, you who say, "Today or tomorrow we will go to this or that city, spend a year there, carry on business and make money." Why, you do not even know what will happen tomorrow. What is your life? You are a mist that appears for a little while and then vanishes.

Instead, you ought to say, "If it is the Lord's will, we will live and do this or that." (James 4:13–15)

The book of Proverbs is full of wisdom for daily living. It gives examples of actions and consequences. Some actions that we take have consequences that reach far into the future. Some attitudes determine misfortune or reward. The guidance we gain from reading Proverbs can help us avoid bad decisions and give direction for good decisions. There are thirty-one chapters that can be read a chapter per day in a month.

God created us and has even given us the Bible, a manual to know how to live in such a way that brings benefits to us and glory to Him. His main purpose for creating us is for fellowship with Him on a personal basis. It is more than we can comprehend that the Creator of the universe desires to have a relationship with each of us, even while we are living on this earth. Oh, the anguish Jesus endured to pay the price to reconcile sinful mankind to the heavenly Father so that anyone who believes in the Son has everlasting life. From Genesis through Revelation, the Bible is a gift to us that explains His glorious plan.

> For God has not appointed us to [incur His] wrath—He did not select us to condemn us —but [that we might] obtain [His] salvation through our Lord Jesus Christ, the Messiah, who died for us so that whether we are still alive or are dead [at Christ's appearing] we might live together with Him and share His life. (1 Thessalonians 5:9–10 AMP)

What joy it is to be able to experience our Lord's presence, even now. He speaks to us through Scripture and true pastors and teachers. Also, the Holy Spirit gives us a knowing in our spirit with promptings to carry out our heavenly Father's will as well as through our conscience. If we refuse to listen, there are major consequences. Don't blame God! If you choose to continue going down a road that is full of pits that the Bible identifies as sin, in thought or action, don't whine about the results. That is not the Lord's will for you. We are given the free will to choose the path we take. God is patient, but there is a point that He will give you over to your own devices and allow you to reap the consequences. Society does not call these things sin or wrong, but instead, equality and rights and freedoms. The Bible plainly tells us that the repercussions are a result of sin and disobedience. Just because society gives approval, it does not change the fact that it is sin. Some of our courts have ruled that we are to embrace wrong as right. Even our schools are directed to teach tolerance of sin. In the Bible, it is predicted that this would happen. Just because it is the twenty-first century, it does not change God's instructions to us that were written over thousands of years. God is holy and will not tolerate sin, disobedience, and rebellion forever. "But the plans of the LORD stand forever, the purposes of his heart through all generations" (Psalm 33:11).

No matter how far away from God you have strayed, He can still orchestrate everything in your life, combining the happy times and bad times to create a beautiful tapestry for His glory and your good. Even if I am just a knotted thread on the back side of His tapestry, I am thrilled to be a part of His beautiful plan. Return to Him and away from sin. Like the prodigal son's father, He will welcome you back with open arms.

"He who believes in the Son has everlasting life; and he who does not believe the Son shall not see life, but the wrath of God abides on him" (John 3:36 NKJV).

That is the future! We must have the righteousness of Christ. The Bible tells us that our own righteousness is like filthy rags. We can never be good enough or do enough good to deserve eternity with God. It is only through the sacrificial blood of Christ that we can receive His righteousness and stand before Holy God. Thanks be to Sovereign God for making a way for us. We must repent, turn away from our sinful ways, and receive this wonderful gift of our Savior.

> If we claim to be without sin, we deceive ourselves and the truth is not in us. If we confess our sins, he is faithful and just and will forgive us our sins and purify us from all unrighteousness. If we claim we have not sinned, we make him out to be a liar and his word has no place in our lives. (1 John 1:8–10)

Thank you, dear Lord, for Your constant presence in our lives. Help us to hear Your whispers of love to us. Open our eyes to see Your blessings for us each day, and know that You are already in the future, so we have no reason to be anxious about it. That is why there is no knob on the Future/Tomorrow door. You graciously only give us one day at a time. Help us to live in Today and leave the Past and the Future in Your perspective. You did not create us to handle the whole realm at once. Jesus, please remind us that You are the same yesterday, today, and forever.

Chapter 12

In Christ Jesus

The promises given in the Bible come through our personal relationship with our Lord and Savior, Jesus Christ. If you have not done so already, Today is the day to receive Christ as your Savior and Lord. According to Scripture, every person is a sinner and separated from God.

"See to it, brothers, that none of you has a sinful, unbelieving heart that turns away from the living God. But encourage one another daily, as long as it is called Today, so that none of you may be hardened by sin's deceitfulness" (Hebrews 3:12–13).

"For the wages of sin is death; but the gift of God is eternal life in Christ Jesus our Lord" (Romans 6:23).

"For God so loved the world that He gave his only begotten Son, that whoever believes in Him should not perish but have everlasting life" (John 3:16 NKJV).

"This righteousness from God comes through faith in Jesus Christ to all who believe. There is no difference, for all have sinned and fall short of the glory of God, and are justified freely by his grace through the redemption that came by Christ Jesus" (Romans 3:22–24).

"If you confess with your mouth, 'Jesus is Lord,' and believe in your heart that God raised him from the dead, you will be saved. For it is with your heart that you believe and are justified, and it is with your mouth that you confess and are saved" (Romans 10:9–10).

"If we confess our sins, he is faithful and just and will forgive us our sins and purify us from all unrighteousness" (1 John 1:9).

"I tell you, now is the time of God's favor, now is the day of salvation" (2 Corinthians 6:2b).

If you would like to receive Jesus Christ as your Lord and Savior right now, you can pray, in your own words, something like this:

Dear heavenly Father, I know I am a sinner. I am sorry for all the things I have done wrong. I choose to turn away from my sins. I believe that Jesus is Lord. I believe that He is Your Son and that He died for my sins on the cross. I believe that You raised Him from the dead. I want to receive You, Jesus, as my Savior and Lord and have a personal relationship with You. Please come into my heart, forgive me, and transform my life to honor You.

Thank you, Father, for this new life in Christ and for everlasting life.

When you honestly pray that prayer, God works a miracle in you, and you are reborn.

> Praise be to the God and Father of our Lord Jesus Christ! In his great mercy he has given us a new birth into a living hope through the resurrection of Jesus Christ from the dead, and into an inheritance that can never perish, spoil or fade—kept in heaven for you, who through faith are shielded by God's power until the coming of the salvation that is ready to be revealed in the last time. (1 Peter 1:3–5)

Welcome into the family of God!

"Being confident in this, that he who began a good work in you will carry it on to completion until the day of Christ Jesus" (Philippians 1:6).

> Nevertheless I am continually with You;
> You hold me by my right hand.

You will guide me with your counsel,

And afterward receive me to glory.

Whom have I in heaven but You?

And there is none upon earth that I desire besides You.

My flesh and my heart fail;

But God is the strength of my heart and
my portion forever.

(Psalm 73:23–26 NKJV)

Our dear God has given us so many wonderful promises in the Bible. I know, we do not deserve any of them. The Savior's love is so great that He patiently waits for us to come to Him. We are so burdened down trying to manage life on our own. Jesus wants to replace fear of the future with peace. Remember, the Lord of lords loves you.

> You will guard him and keep him in perfect and constant peace whose mind [both its inclination and its character] is stayed on You, because he commits himself to You, leans on You and hopes confidently in You. So trust in the Lord—commit yourself to Him, lean on Him, hope confidently in Him—for ever; for the Lord God is an everlasting Rock—the Rock of ages. (Isaiah 26:3–4 AMP)

The real peace we long for comes from trusting the Creator and through submission to Him. We must always pray for God's will to be done. Rest in His sovereignty.

When sitting on my patio watching the birds and butterflies, I am blessed by the wonder of creation. The butterfly makes me think of salvation and the rapture. The caterpillar is transformed, during its time in a cocoon, into a beautiful butterfly. Who could do that except God Almighty? Our time on earth is a span of time when the Holy Spirit is transforming us on the inside after we have received Jesus as our own personal Savior and Lord. When Jesus returns to take us with Him, we don't know how we will look. I am sure the transformation will be complete and glorious, like the example of the butterfly.

> For I am convinced that neither death nor life, neither angels nor demons, neither the present nor the future, nor any powers, neither height nor depth nor anything else in all creation, will be able to separate us from the love of God that is in Christ Jesus our Lord. (Romans 8:38–39)

For anyone who has prayed the sinner's prayer, receiving Christ as your Savior and Lord, keep in mind that Satan is not happy about anyone turning their life over to Jesus. He does not want to give up control. You can expect challenges from him. He will try to convince you that nothing has changed.

The more Scripture you know, the easier it is to resist Satan. You can put on the armor of God as described in Ephesians 6:10–18.

Don't hesitate, get into a Bible-believing church. Spend time daily in prayer and Scripture. Take off the old self and walk in this new life in Christ. The Bible is our instruction manual as well as it teaches us about the greatness of God's love for each of us.

Chapter 13
Letting Go

Why do we find it so hard to let go, to let go of the past, let go of the future, and even to let go of responsibilities that are not personally ours to carry? We hang on to ourselves and our possessions. All tangibles and intangibles belong to God. The past is gone, and the present and future are in His control. The great thing is that He loves us and wants us to be dependent on Him. We are not the owner of ourselves or anything we possess. We are stewards, administrators of all He has provided.

You, O Lord, give us everything we need in the physical, mental, and spiritual realms. Trials are allowed to come upon us to strengthen and mature us. You convict us of our sins to call us to repentance. Great is Your faithfulness in drawing near to us as we draw near to You.

Help us accept the things we cannot change, letting go of them to Your care. Give us the grace to change what is our responsibility to change. Give us Your wisdom to discern what is beyond our realm of responsibility and when to let go. Help us to trust You to work out Your will and plans.

Letting go of loved ones is an enormous thing to do. We finally must realize that we can't control their issues, decisions, or conditions. It's a matter of loving and caring about them, but not caretaking. Their situation is usually the consequence of their own choices and actions. Turn them over to our loving heavenly Father, and get out of the way. God knows best what it will take to bring them to reality and loves them beyond measure.

Only You, Lord, can reach into the depth of their hearts and rescue them from their own self-destructive ways. It is not abandoning them; instead, relinquishing them and trusting You.

Dear Lord, sometimes I think we are afraid that You won't work things out according to our expectations.

Jesus' followers expected Him to become their king on earth and rescue them from the rule of the Romans. That is what the Jews were celebrating on Palm Sunday.

"They took palm branches and went out to meet him, shouting, "Hosanna!" "Blessed is he who comes in the name of the Lord!" "Blessed is the King of Israel!" (John 12:13).

They did not understand that His kingdom was not of this world, as He told Pilate.

"Jesus said, "My kingdom is not of this world. If it were, my servants would fight to prevent my arrest by the Jews. But now my kingdom is from another place" (John 18:36).

God's plan is not limited to that time in history. His plan includes all His people before that time, all the way into our time and the future. We are fortunate to have Scripture that gives us the bigger picture. It shows us history, promises, fulfilled prophesy, and prophesy yet to be fulfilled. As His children, we look forward to His return when He takes us to be with Him. There is eternal suffering for those who refuse to accept the most precious gift of God; His Son.

Why, oh why, would we hesitate to let go and entrust everything to Him? He is sovereign. He is over all. He is so incredibly patient with us.

"The LORD is gracious and compassionate, slow to anger and rich in love" (Psalm 145:8).

What more could He do to convince us of His love for us? He gave His only begotten Son to take our sins upon Himself in order to free us from sin and even the guilt of it. Jesus paid the debt He did not owe and paid the debt we could not pay.

Our heavenly Father loves us that much and desires fellowship with us. That is too big for me to grasp. We can't understand the enormity of His great love. As humans, that unconditional love is more than we can fathom. By faith, we can believe and give ourselves over to Him. He tells us to bring our burdens to Him.

"Come to me, all you who are weary and burdened, and I will give you rest. Take my yoke upon you and learn from me, for I am gentle and humble in heart, and you will find rest for you souls. For my yoke is easy and my burden is light" (Matthew 11:28–30).

I picture a big ox in the yoke on one side and a sheep in the yoke on the other side. Guess who is carrying the burden. Oh, little sheep, why do we insist on carrying our burdens ourselves when our dear Lord wants to carry them for us? Is it pride in self-sufficiency or arrogance? We think, That's okay, Lord, I've got this! But our sufficiency is in God's sufficiency. He gives us abilities and talents. When we receive His power and grace, those things can be developed and bring glory to Him. We have the joy, and He gets the praise. Thank you, Jesus!

I think I will take a praise break. I feel like walking outside at the end of the hall and singing songs of praise and worship to our wonderful God. See those music notes going up in the air? How refreshing to my soul.

As I get older, the things of this world are less and less valuable to me. I don't need a lot of stuff to be content. To have the latest and greatest thing that comes on the market does not appeal to me. My desire is to know Jesus more intimately. Just think, we can lose everything, as some people have, whether possessions, relationships, or even loved ones. But we still always have our Lord to sustain and comfort us. In our lifetime, we may face major persecution before Jesus comes to take us to Himself; however, He promises never to leave us or forsake us. He will give us the grace to endure, so we are to let go of worry. He holds the future in His hands.

Is there anything in your life that keeps you from loving God with your whole heart, your mind, and strength? That is the first commandment. "And you shall love the Lord your God with all your [mind and] heart, and with your entire being, and with all your might" (Deuteronomy 6:5 AMP).

You can ask the Holy Spirit to reveal to you any attachments to the world that are holding you back. Ask Him to help you to let go in order to have the freedom that total commitment to God brings. Our identity is not in our accomplishments or failures, but instead, our identity is in Christ. We live in this world; however, we are not of this world. It is difficult to live in this world without being caught up in the things of this world.

In the book of Daniel, we are given the account of young Daniel and his three friends when they were taken captive from Jerusalem into the pagan culture of Babylon. Their convictions and commitment to God had already been formed. All four were intelligent and anointed by God. They continued to practice their allegiance to God, even though they were taught the culture of the Babylonians in order to serve in the king's service. Daniel was able, by God's intervention, to tell the king what his dream was and what it meant. This greatly impressed the king to the point that he said, "Your God is the God of gods and Lord of kings and a revealer of mysteries, for you were able to reveal this mystery!" (Daniel 2:47). Then, the king made Daniel ruler over the whole province of Babylon. At Daniel's request, the king appointed the three friends to be over the affairs of the province of Babylon.

The king had a huge image of gold made and commanded everyone to bow down to the image. Anyone who refused to bow down to the image would be thrown into the burning fiery furnace. Word got back to the king that the three Jewish friends, Shadrach, Meshach, and Abednego, would not worship the image. The king was furious! He told them, "But if you do not worship it, you will be thrown immediately into a blazing furnace. Then what god will be able to rescue you from my hand?" (Daniel 3:15b).

> The three responded, 'If we are thrown into the blazing furnace, the God we serve is able to save us from it, and he will rescue us from your hand, O king. But even if he does not, we want you to know, O king, that we will not serve your gods or worship the image of gold you have set up.' (Daniel 3:17–18)

When the three were bound and thrown into the furnace, the king jumped to his feet and exclaimed that he saw four men walking around in the fire, unbound and unharmed, and that the fourth man looked like a son of the gods. The king shouted for the three to come out. Then, the king exclaimed, "Praise be to the God of Shadrach, Meshach and Abednego, who sent his angel and rescued his servants! They trusted in him and defied the king's command and were willing to give up their lives rather than serve or worship any god except their own God" (Daniel 3:28).

There are many signs and wonders recorded, including God shutting the mouths of the lions when Daniel was thrown into the den. You can read all about it in the book of Daniel. God's mighty power was demonstrated through the faithfulness and trust of these four young men.

Daniel and his friends did not waiver from centering their lives around the true God. They did not give in to the culture of Babylon or compromise by serving or worshiping the idol gods.

In our own culture, we don't set up a golden image, but even so, there are idols all around us. Whatever we set before us that we focus on or make a priority of and marginalize our God, that becomes a god to you. Ask God to examine your heart and show you what is taking His rightful place. Don't make excuses. Check on yourself. On what or who are you giving yourself to instead of God? It may even be "Self."

Let go of these idols. Confess these distractions as sin, and ask the Lord to help you turn from them. Then you can focus on the purposes that God has specifically for you. That will bring peace to you and glory to Him.

Another area that we must let go of is our expectations. For example, when things don't go the way we thought they should, or our loved ones do not fulfill our expectations of them. We have all experienced disappointment when we let ourselves down, especially when we feel we have failed our heavenly Father.

We can take these unfulfilled expectations, disappointments, and failures to our Lord and release those yellow balloons to Him. When we confess our sins to Him, He forgives us. He knows our weaknesses and gives us His strength as we depend on Him. Great is our God!

In the matter of forgiving others, we must pray for wisdom. After we have forgiven a person who has violated our trust and let go of the offense, we must pray for wisdom in going forward in a relationship with them. Has that person shown that they have truly repented? Matthew 3:8 states, "Produce fruit in keeping with repentance." If their attitude or actions do not show that they have changed, then perhaps you should distance yourself from them to prevent further hurt. We must forgive because God has forgiven us our wrongs. We just need to love some people from a distance.

> No good tree bears bad fruit, nor does a bad tree bear good fruit. Each tree is recognized by its own fruit. People do not pick figs from thornbushes, or grapes from briers. The good man brings good things out of the good stored up in his heart, and the evil man brings evil things

out of the evil stored up in his heart. For out of the overflow of his heart his mouth speaks. (Luke 6:43–45)

There was a time in my life when it was not possible to distance myself, so I had to ask God to love through me. It felt like my own love had been wrung out of me. I felt so overwhelmed and unqualified for the situation I was in. But the Lord was good. He arranged occasional reprieves for me to have some time out of the stress. Plus, I began painting again, which was joyful and relaxing for me. I don't understand how anyone can get through ongoing negative circumstances without the Lord. I stayed committed to the Lord and the role I was in. During those years, I had not yet learned how to apply the principles that are presented in the *Today, No Knobs, Letting Go* painting.

I hope this book can help you understand and apply these principles so that you can avert a lot of pain and sorrow for yourself and others.

Today I had an "opportunity" to apply the principle of letting go. I am so proud of my husband because he has restarted walking in the neighborhood for exercise. I told him I would like to buy a bright safety vest for him so the traffic could easily spot him. Wasn't that sweet and thoughtful of me? He said he would like one that zips and has pockets. I spent the morning looking through the computer to find which store had what he wanted. I gave my time and effort, right?

There was a return I had to make at the hardware store. I asked him if he would like to go. As we were about to leave home, I said, "Perhaps that hardware store would have a vest you would like."

So, while I was making the return, he went to another department to check if they had vests. I joined him there. He said, "Let's go across the street where they sell bicycles to look for a vest." I asked if they did not have any where we were. He said, "I don't think they have any here."

Me, "Did you ask?"

"No, but let's go to the other store." Off we go.

The clerks in the other store looked all over and finally located a skimpy half vest. On my phone, I looked up the hardware store where we had just been, and it showed a big selection of vests. I thought we were going back across the street to ask where the vests were located. But my husband said that I could go to the hardware store and see about one for myself; he had decided he did not want to spend his money on one. He did not want one; he had done without one all his life and did not need one! I opted to go home.

Who said anything about him buying it? Remember this morning when I told him I would like to buy a vest for him? Then I spent my morning researching for the kind he wanted.

Anyway, back to the principle of letting go. I had to catch myself from giving in to being hurt and angry. I could tell my body was tensing up. I thought about the yellow balloons. Okay, I have a choice to allow myself to get bent out of shape, or I can pray and walk to the end of the hall and let the balloon go. I don't have to let this ruin my day. I must resist trying to be helpful to him. He has a right to do things his own way. However, he could have told me this morning that he did not want a vest! It just makes me feel unappreciated. Oh, well.

After praying, I chose to let it go. I'm sure he could write some pages about my shortcomings.

Time for a break. I am going to ride my bike around the neighborhood. It is a beautiful day. It relaxes me to go for a spin in the fresh air.

Remember James 1:2–4, "Consider it pure joy, my brothers

whenever you face trials of many kinds, because you know that the testing of your faith develops perseverance. Perseverance must finish its work so that you may be mature and complete, not lacking anything."

I do feel joy. The test had a purpose, and it proved to me how applying what I had learned about letting go really did remove the negative feelings. It freed me to enjoy the rest of the day with my husband.

It was necessary for me, also, to remember that years ago, I had consciously decided and committed to forgiving ahead of time any offense that would occur in my life. Therefore, forgiveness was not a decision I had to make today. That was already done.

My husband and I are on the "same page" quite often, but other times, it seems we are from different planets. Sometimes the meaning of my words becomes scrambled somewhere between my mouth and his brain. Can you relate to that observation in your experience?

Paul wrote to the Philippians while he was in prison in Rome. "Rejoice in the Lord always. I will say it again: Rejoice! Let your gentleness be evident to all. The Lord is near" (Philippians 4:4–5).

> Finally, brothers, whatever is true, whatever is noble, whatever is right, whatever is pure, whatever is lovely, whatever is admirable—if anything is excellent or praiseworthy—think about such things. Whatever you have learned or received or heard from me, or seen in me—put it into practice. And the God of peace will be with you. (Philippians 4:8–9)

That is the challenge; practice!

This morning, in a phone conversation with a friend, we

were talking about how we are still learning how to apply the Bible to our lives at this point in life. We both know a lot of Scripture and have been in church all our lives. We both enjoy the presence of the Holy Spirit. Perhaps part of the problem is that we have not taken the time to practice these principles on a regular basis when an occasion arises. We kind of go into auto-pilot with our emotions instead of consciously choosing to do things God's way. My desire is to automatically, habitually respond in His will and way. Then, we truly can enjoy His peace.

Chapter 14

Surrender

This is a major challenge, letting go of our Self. Our biggest idol is probably Self. Following Jesus is an individual surrender and commitment. When Jesus called His disciples, they dropped everything and followed Him. He does not call everyone to be in public ministry, but He does call each of us to follow Him each day, denying ourselves.

"Then he said to them all: 'If anyone would come after me, he must deny himself and take up his cross daily and follow me. For whoever wants to save his life will lose it, but whoever loses his life for me will save it'" (Luke 9:23–24).

"Anyone who loves his father or mother more than me is not worthy of me; anyone who loves his son or daughter more than me is not worthy of me, and anyone who does not take his cross and follow me is not worthy of me" (Matthew 10:37–38).

How can our Lord take me or you on the path that He has for us individually if we do not surrender ourselves to Him? How can our heavenly Father accomplish His purposes through us if we refuse to let go of all and follow Him?

The time comes that we must surrender our loved ones to God. We always love them and lift them up in prayer; however, we must give up our own dreams for them. It is so hard to release our expectations and disappointments.

Our whole family was involved in church wherever we lived. My children grew up being active in the children and youth ministries. They both accepted Christ and were baptized at an early age. I continue to release those yellow balloons as I commit them into our Father's hands and heart. My hope is in the Holy Spirit to soften their hearts and restore fellowship with Him.

I have known people who have given up on God because He did not come through with their own agenda. Many hold on to sin and expect God to bless them anyway.

In Hebrews 12:1, it says, "Let us throw off everything that hinders, and the sin that so easily entangles, and let us run with perseverance the race marked out for us."

"Since they hated knowledge and did not choose to fear the LORD, since they would not accept my advice and spurned my rebuke, they will eat the fruit of their ways and be filled with the fruit of their schemes" (Proverbs 1:29–31).

"If anyone will not welcome you or listen to your words, shake the dust off your feet when you leave that home or town" (Matthew 10:14).

When we surrender our grown-up loved ones to God and stop wearing ourselves out trying to help them, there are benefits for them and us. For us, we can now have freedom from the distractions and emotional stress of their continual chaos so that we can go forward with what the Lord wants to do with our lives. For them, they hopefully will learn to lean on the Lord and renew their relationship with Him, which includes all the benefits of being God's children. We are not abandoning them, just letting them be adults without our supervision. They may never see the sacrifices we have made for them. However, we must never bring up that subject. They may disconnect from communication, but their relationship with the Lord is certainly far more valuable than their relationship with us. That is between them and God. Of course, we continue to pray and thank God for His love and patience with all of us.

"Pointing to his disciples, he said, 'Here are my mother and my brothers. For whoever does the will of my Father in heaven is my brother and sister and mother'" (Matthew 12:49–50).

"So then, each of us will give an account of himself to God" (Romans 14:12).

It is necessary to remember that God is God, and I am not. Only He knows what it takes to bring people back to Him. We love them and do what we can, but there is a time to let go and let God. It has taken me years to come to the realization and resolve to relinquish them to Him.

"Listen my son, to your father's instruction and do not forsake your mother's teaching. They will be a garland to grace your head and a chain to adorn your neck" (Proverbs 1:8–9).

We must do our part as parents but then surrender our grown children into the faithful hands of our heavenly Father. They are responsible for their own choices. They can choose to serve the Lord or not. We must get out of the way and let God deal with them as He sees fit. With young children and teens, we must lovingly help them learn about the consequences of their own responsibilities and choices, whether good or bad. Many times, I failed at that! I rescued them instead of allowing them to experience the natural consequences of irresponsible behavior. I would fill in the gap to avert the consequences. That was relying on me to be responsible instead of being accountable themselves. This kind of intervention continued into their adulthood.

In our society today, it seems that many children and teens assume that they are in charge. They do what they please as many parents are too occupied to train them. Many parents are not self-disciplined themselves and don't set the example or training for their children to be respectful of other people or property of others. Everyone seems overburdened with so much stuff and distractions. Too much time on entertainment and technology can rob children of playing outside, playing together, and learning social skills. Creativity can lose appeal and may not be encouraged. Chores shared in the family can teach responsibility. Many video games are full of violence which can influence behavior. However, while the kids are occupied with electronics, they are out of the parents' way, so the preoccupied parent can accomplish what needs to be done or escape into their own corner of respite. It is easy to lose hours browsing on our phones or on the computer. I have caught myself wasting time reading endless posts.

TV, movies, and video games are areas that have evolved and desensitized us to tolerate obscene talk and sinful behavior on screen. I have heard, "Well, it is just an actor portraying the scene; I am not committing the sin." Whether it be murder or lust, etc., that is portrayed in the film, Jesus tells us in Matthew 5:27, "You have heard that it was said, 'Do not commit adultery.' But I tell you that anyone who looks at a woman lustfully has already committed adultery with her in his heart."

Just because we are not physically involved in the script, isn't it also desensitizing our children and us to accept as normal, condone, and possibly live out that influence? Those glamorous characters become role models.

Isn't that counter-productive as parents try to train up their children in God's ways? Look around at our current culture today, and you will see the answer! It is up to each individual to set limits and priorities for ourselves and the children to help them develop self-control and perseverance to delay gratification. Children need and are more secure with boundaries in many areas. It also helps them to build character to resist peer pressure.

Remember Daniel and his friends were teenagers when they were taken captive in Babylon. At that age, they were already strong in character and resolved to keep their allegiance to God.

Quality time and communication get lost in our overcrowded lives and disconnect us from our own family members.

Oh God, please help us to align our priorities and boundaries with Yours. Show us what things are robbing us of our time and devotion to You and each other.

Satan's trick is to rob us. Resist, realign! Take time for joy and praise. Let go of the things that are not God's best for you. Even some good things must go to make room for God's best.

Many households are up to their eyeballs in debt. We don't need the latest and greatest of everything that comes out on the market or just because someone else you know has one. God promises to supply our needs. Maybe the pandemic has caused a lot of people to reevaluate needs as opposed to wants that run up credit card debt. God gives instructions throughout the Bible about finances. Proverbs 22:26–27 states, "Do not be a man who strikes hands in pledge or puts up security for debts; if you lack the means to pay, your very bed will be snatched from under you."

In so many homes, one of the parents is missing, either physically or emotionally. If you read the first books of the Bible, you will see how seriously God takes the responsibilities of the parents and the children. The book of Proverbs is filled with instructions for parents, small children, and grown sons and daughters. All throughout the New Testament are commands and instructions for our actions, attitudes, and responsibilities.

> Children, obey your parents in the Lord, for this is right. 'Honor your father and mother'—which is the first commandment with a promise—'that it may go well with you and that you may enjoy long life on the earth.'
>
> Fathers, do not exasperate your children, instead bring them up in the training and instruction of the Lord. (Ephesians 6:1–4)

"Children, obey your parents in everything, for this pleases the Lord. Fathers, do not embitter your children, or they will become discouraged" (Colossians 3:20–21).

"My son, do not make light of the Lord's discipline, and do not lose heart when he rebukes you, because the Lord disciplines those he loves, and he punishes everyone he accepts as a son. Endure hardship as discipline; God is treating you as sons" (Hebrews 12:5b–7a).

> Moreover, we have all had human fathers who disciplined us and we respected them for it. How much more should we submit to the Father of our spirits and live! Our fathers disciplined us for a little while as they thought best; but God disciplines us for our good, that we may share in his holiness. No discipline seems pleasant at the time, but painful. Later on, however, it produces a harvest of righteousness and peace for those who have been trained by it. (Hebrews 12:9–11)

Discipline is to be done in love with the aim of building character, self-discipline, and respect. Remember to exercise self-control over your anger and frustration.

"Train a child in the way he should go, and when he is old he will not turn from it" (Proverbs 22:6).

Let your life be a testimony of love and trust that is worthy of your children's respect.

Children are a gift to a marriage. They are a mixture of blessings and challenges. We need all the guidance we can get from the Bible, our own conversations with the Father in heaven, and in the environment of a church family. We can learn from other parents' successes and failures, even in the Bible.

I have seen a lot of fathers abdicate their position as godly heads of household to their wives. Most wives in the twenty-first century work outside the home. Especially with children, this means, without help, she is already handling two jobs. Then if the husband relies on her to manage and juggle everything else, it is too much! He can become another dependent on her. The core of their marriage can erode with this arrangement.

The Bible addresses husbands and fathers a lot. God expects the man to take the position of being the godly leader of the home, not leave a void and expect the wife to fill it. This is an easy trap for a wife to fall into because it is back to "somebody has to do it." But then, she is usurping his role, which God has established. Late in my first marriage, I learned that women must resist stepping in when the husband does not step up to the plate and practice his obligations. I remember seeing red flags before we married. My perspective was that he was just lacking in self-confidence. I was too enamored to heed the signs that he was not mature enough yet for marriage. Really, neither of us was mature enough for marriage. I thought I could build his self-esteem. Right! It never occurred to me that there were underlying reasons for his dependent nature. I knew he needed encouragement and appreciation, but I had no idea of the depth of his problems until much later. Nobody should ever go into marriage thinking they can change or fix their fiancé. It is not going to happen. We can only change ourselves by submission to God.

First Timothy chapter 3 gives a description of a godly man. Proverbs 31:10–31 gives a model for a godly woman. The Bible tells husbands and wives how to treat each other.

"Husbands, love your wives, just as Christ loved the church and gave himself up for her to make her holy, cleansing her by the washing with water through the word" (Ephesians 5:25–26).

"Wives, submit to your husbands as to the Lord. For the husband is the head of the wife as Christ is the head of the church, his body, of which he is the Savior" (Ephesians 5:22–23).

"Submit to one another out of reverence for Christ" (Ephesians 5:21).

"However, each one of you also must love his wife as he loves himself, and the wife must respect her husband" (Ephesians 5:33).

When both are fulfilling their God-ordained roles, it makes it easier for the spouse to fulfill his or hers. If the core of the marriage is solid, with both spouses living their respective positions in Christ, there is a great foundation. God's plan is for children to live in a family of two parents; man is father, and woman is mother. Genesis 1:26–28 explains this basic.

In our current society, there are a lot of men and women who have not had a godly example to follow. But we are all accountable to our heavenly Father, who gives us guidance as we study His Word, attend a Bible-teaching church, and fellowship with other believers. We can encourage and be supportive of each other. It requires cooperation of both spouses in a marriage.

Every couple has their own scenario. I'm passing on things I have learned through my experiences, hindsight, and seeking God's wisdom. Plus, I have learned from other folks' experiences.

The basic step for any person is to surrender to Jesus everything, everybody, and ourselves, which opens the way to enjoy a wonderful personal relationship with Him.

Another aspect of surrender is to learn not to be self-defensive. Some people seem to be naturally oppositional. If you suggest something to them, they immediately veto the idea. You can ask them to do something or go somewhere with you. The automatic answer is no. Even though, later, they may come through for you.

I bet you have someone in mind right now.

You may even considerately do something for them, yet

they accuse you of an ulterior motive. Case in point: It was a very hot day. I went outside to ask my husband if he was ready for lunch. He said, "I know when I need to stop working. You don't have to tell me."

My feeling of frustration and aggravation kicked in. But I caught myself and said, "I only asked you if you were ready for lunch." Then I went on about my business instead of continuing the conversation in my own self-defense. I'm learning that it just is not worth getting all tensed up physically or mentally, which would impair my Today. I know he does not like to be disturbed when he is in the middle of a project or task. I guess he took it as me being bossy.

It is amazing that writing this book is helping me to apply the things that I am sharing with you, which is making me a calmer person. I appreciate the Holy Spirit reminding me when I start to react instead of keeping Today in focus, remembering that there are no knobs on the Past and Future doors, and letting go of the worry balloons with prayer and worship, plus anything else that interferes with devotion to our wonderful God.

It is a matter of practical application of some of the principles of God's Word. In Zechariah 4:6b, the Bible says, "'Not by might nor by power, but by my Spirit,' says the LORD Almighty." It is the Holy Spirit that enables us to remember and practice the instructions that are taught in the Bible.

"Jesus replied, If anyone loves me, he will obey my teaching. My Father will love him, and we will come to him and make our home with him. He who does not love me will not obey my teaching" (John 14:23–24).

> But the Counselor, the Holy Spirit, whom the Father will send in my name, will teach you all things and will remind you of everything I have said to you. Peace I

leave with you; my peace I give you. I do not give to you as the world gives. Do not let your hearts be troubled and do not be afraid. (John 14:26–27)

Thank You, dear Father. You are so good and patient, full of love, mercy, and grace. Thank You for all the gifts You lavish upon us. Thank You for Your promises and constant care. Thank You for giving us eternal life with You. Help us to live honoring You by our obedience and surrendering all to You. May You be glorified in all the earth.

Chapter 15

Deception

You know Satan is an expert at deception. When we are faithful to be in God's Word and prayer, it prepares us to be discerning when Satan tells his lies. As time gets shorter before our Jesus comes to take His church in the rapture, Satan is working even harder to convince all people to turn from God and engage in the "freedoms" that he offers by rejecting God's ways. Those "freedoms" are crossing the boundaries that God has established for our welfare. It is breaking the relationship with our loving God to follow the ways of the world in self-indulgence, sinful behavior, and attitudes.

In John 8:43, Satan is referred to as the father of lies. His pride is exposed as he proclaims what his intentions are. The following passage refers to the pride of the Babylonian kings, who are compared to Satan.

"And you said in your heart, I will ascend to Heaven: I will exalt my throne above the stars of God; I will sit upon the mount of assembly in the uttermost north; I will ascend above the heights of the clouds, I will make myself like the Most High" (Isaiah 14:13–14).

I may be criticized for some of the things that I address in this chapter. However, I stand on the truths presented in the Bible. I do not mean to accuse or judge anyone of anything, but instead, to point out the deception that many have fallen into. We are all subjected to the influence of Satan's lies. We constantly need to stay on guard.

"All Scripture is God-breathed and is useful for teaching, rebuking, correcting and training in righteousness, so that the man of God may be thoroughly equipped for every good work" (2 Timothy 3:16–17).

In my lifetime, I have seen the removal of prayer and the Bible from public schools and the removal of the Ten Commandments in many places. These actions and many laws in this generation have changed the conscience of our nation. You see what has happened to our society, our schools, and our universities. Like by a pied piper, our children are being led away. They are told to be tolerant and politically correct. Many of these institutions that formerly educated students with integrity and character are no longer tolerant of virtues and spiritual values. That is evident in the lack of self-respect, respect for others, work ethics, conscientiousness, self-discipline, etc., in much of our society.

Even many churches have centered on entertainment instead of worshiping God in spirit and in truth. Some denominations compromise and reject the Bible as the inerrant and inspired Word of God. There are some new translations and paraphrases which distort the truth.

> I am astonished that you are so quickly deserting the one who called you by the grace of Christ and are turning to a different gospel—which is really no gospel at all. Evidently some people are throwing you into confusion and are trying to pervert the gospel of Christ. (Galatians 1:6–7)

Where is the sanctity of life and marriage as defined in Scripture?

"So God created man in his own image, in the image of God he created him; male and female he created them. God blessed them and said to them, 'Be fruitful and increase in number; fill the earth and subdue it'" (Genesis 1:27–28a).

"Haven't you read," he replied, "that at the beginning the Creator 'made them male and female,' and said, 'For this reason a man will leave his father and mother and be united to his wife, and the two will become one flesh'? So they are no longer two, but one. Therefore what God has joined together, let no man separate." (Matthew 19:4–6)

Marriage, the sacred institution ordained by our heavenly Father, today is being defiled, devalued, and dishonored. I know this may step on some toes. However, it is necessary to know the truth in order to reject the lies. Our society has been so desensitized and deceived in this area.

Engaging in sexual intercourse before marriage and living together before marriage has become the norm for a lot of people. But it is an insult to our Creator. It is totally out of His will. How can blessings from God be expected when living in opposition to His mandates? In this self-gratification experience, who is thinking about the welfare of the children who can come as a result of this activity? Where is the commitment to provide family security?

This union is not like taking a car for a test drive before you decide to commit to purchasing it! Marriage is a holy estate based on the kind of love that embraces commitment and self-sacrifice. It has bonds so strong that the two are as one. It is based on purity for each other, faithfulness, and devotion.

Love is patient, love is kind. It does not envy, it does not boast, it is not proud. It is not rude, it is not self-seeking, it is not easily angered, it keeps no record of wrongs. Love does not delight in evil but rejoices with the truth. It always protects, always trusts, always hopes, always perseveres. (1 Corinthians 13:4–7)

"Do not be yoked together with unbelievers" (2 Corinthians 6:14a). "What does a believer have in common with an unbeliever?" (2 Corinthians 6:15b).

"Marriage should be honored by all, and the marriage bed kept pure, for God will judge the adulterer and all the sexually immoral" (Hebrews 13:4).

Just because society approves, it does not make it okay. Each person is accountable to God.

Many people have been lulled into apathy as each is absorbed in their own perimeter, escaping into entertainment, work, or whatever to block out dealing with the reality of subversive activity that has been going on for years. Now, it is not even subtle. It is blatantly expressed in our government actions that are taking away our true freedoms and replacing them with laws to control and take over our lives. There is a mass of organized groups of people who want to eliminate God from our nation and the world. They want all power and control. Many already have incredible wealth. They do not realize that Satan is using them for his schemes. He caters to mankind's natural selfishness. That is what Satan wants, all power and control. Their agenda is spread through the bias and spinning of the mainline news channels and social media as well as schools, colleges, and universities by deceiving people of the whole truth in order to sway the minds of the public to accept their ideology.

We have also witnessed the disregard for the constitution in our courts. Even the Supreme Court has legislated laws instead of upholding the intentions of the constitution. The Court has misinterpreted and twisted laws in order to conform to the demands of segments of people that force acceptance of immoral behavior that specifically is identified in Scripture.

The Civil Rights laws were intended to eliminate discrimination against people of color and gender (meaning women and men, since God created only two genders). But the courts have exceeded their authority by not interpreting the law as written; instead, they ruled to include people who want their sexual perversion to be accepted and promoted. They want any resistance to be considered a hate crime. The Civil Rights laws have been misused to try to force the acceptance of sexual perversion that is explicitly addressed in Scripture.

There are proposed laws that would force all citizens to incorporate into every segment of our society the ideology of sexual orientation. The scheme is to include these mandates into bills that support other things that are acceptable. These bills are named with titles that sound good. But they are designed to require everyone, every institution, and venue to employ and assimilate people with sexual identity instability issues. They are already in our public schools, influencing our children. It is an assault on biblical values, freedom of speech, and freedom of religion. These mandates take away our right to abstain from going against our conscience. There have already been lawsuits to combat these infringements on our right to reject participating in activities that go against our consciences and religious beliefs. For example, clergy, bakers, and florists who would not in good conscience participate in any part of a same-sex marriage. We should not be expected to compromise our religious values to accommodate deceived people who have fallen for the lies that support their agenda.

These laws are trying to force us to condone and embrace sinful lifestyles. The far-reaching scope is for our whole society to be required to comply with the lies of Satan. That would be in direct opposition to the Bible and science, as both are clear regarding life, marriage, and sexuality.

Although it is not the duty of the Supreme Court to legislate, some laws were set by the Court which are blatantly against Scripture and the Constitution of the United States of America.

Science has declared that life begins at conception. The Bible is clear on gender and marriage. The laws of our nation previously supported these truths.

Women's sports have already been ruined with unfair competition by allowing men with naturally stronger physical strength to compete with women. They are walking away with awards and scholarships that should have gone to biological women.

I am grieved for the people who have embraced the lies and struggle with their sexual identity. However, instead of taking hormones, estrogen, testosterone, or surgery to try to have themselves transgendered, why don't they take the appropriate measures to match the physical anatomy of their bodies? Plus, psychological counseling to help them accept the gender they are.

I can see how teenagers could struggle with these lies because that age is a transition time when boys and girls are experiencing changes in their bodies and hormones as they are becoming adults. It is an awkward time of learning about themselves and adjusting to the new emotions as boys and girls interact with each other. Some can feel inadequate as they compare themselves to their peers. For many reasons, it is a challenging time period. If a girl or boy feels like they don't have what it takes in social interactions with the opposite sex, they may find it easier to associate with their own gender in friendship while they continue to mature. However, with the push for sexual identity ideology, they may begin to question their biological sex. Now, even young children are told that they can choose which gender they want to be! They are allowed to be provided with the process to change from their true gender. Do parents even have a say in that, or does the government force the parents to comply?

Do parents have a say in their pregnant underage daughter's decision to have an abortion?

Parents' responsibilities and rights are being usurped, and

family is being redefined!

It brings tears to my eyes to think of the ramifications of these edicts. And I don't want my tax dollars to pay for these abominations, as it goes against my convictions and conscience. It is in direct rebellion and disobedience to our Creator.

The beginning of the downfall of a nation is the turning away from God.

> Do you not know that the unrighteous and the wrong-doers will not inherit or have any share in the kingdom of God? Do not be deceived (misled); neither the impure and immoral, nor idolaters, nor adulterers, nor those who participate in homosexuality, nor cheats—swindlers and thieves; nor greedy graspers, nor drunkards, nor foulmouthed revilers and slanderers, nor extortioners and robbers will inherit or have any share in the kingdom of God. (1 Corinthians 6:9–10 AMP)

There is hope because of the grace and mercy provided for all who will admit and turn away from their sins and allow the Holy Spirit to help them live a new life in Christ.

> And such some of you were (once). But you were washed clean [purified by a complete atonement for sin and made free from the guilt of sin]; and you were consecrated (set apart, hallowed); and you were justified (pronounced righteous, by trust) in the name of the Lord Jesus Christ and in the (Holy) Spirit of our God. (1 Corinthians 6:11 AMP)

It is possible to repent and turn back to God or come to Him for the first time ever. Jesus made this privilege possible by His death on the cross, taking your sins and guilt on Himself.

Have you received Him as your Savior and Lord? It is possible to wait too late.

In the days of Noah, the people would not repent. When the ark was completed and Noah and his family were inside, at God's timing, He shut the door. All on the outside were drowned as the earth became covered with the great flood.

> For since the creation of the world God's invisible qualities—his eternal power and divine nature—have been clearly seen, being understood from what has been made, so that men are without excuse. For although they knew God, they neither glorified him as God nor gave thanks to him. (Romans 1:20–21a)

> Claiming to be wise, they became fools—professing to be smart, they made simpletons of themselves. And by them the glory and majesty and excellence of the immortal God were exchanged for and represented by images, resembling mortal man and birds and beasts and reptiles.
>
> Therefore God gave them up in the lusts of their [own] hearts to sexual impurity, to the dishonoring of their bodies among themselves, abandoning them to the degrading power of sin. Because they exchanged the truth of God for a lie and worshipped and served the creature rather than the Creator, Who is blessed forever! Amen—so be it.
>
> For this reason God gave them over and abandoned them to vile affections and degrading passions. For their women exchanged their natural function for an unnatural and abnormal one; and the men also turned from natural relations with women and were set ablaze (burned out, consumed) with lust for one another, men committing shameful acts with men and suffering in

their own bodies and personalities the inevitable consequences and penalty of their wrong doing and going
astray, which was [their] fitting retribution.

And so, since they did not see fit to acknowledge God
or approve of Him or consider Him worth the knowing,
God gave them over to a base and condemned mind to
do things not proper or decent but loathsome; until they
were filled—permeated and saturated—with every kind
of unrighteousness. (Romans 1:22–29a AMP)

"Though they are fully aware of God's righteous decree
that those who do such things deserve to die, they not only do
them themselves but approve and applaud others who practice
them" (Romans 1:32 AMP).

We witness that in events like the Gay Pride parades. They
even profane God's rainbow, using it as a symbol of their agenda. In Genesis 9:8–17, the origin of the rainbow is a sign of
the covenant that God made to never again destroy all life on
earth by a flood.

Many people are ignorant of God's Word since it has been
removed from our schools and much of the public square and re-
placed with lies and propaganda. In our country, so far, the Bible
is available to everyone. But some won't seek His wisdom, and
many just don't care!

"How I have been grieved by their adulterous hearts, which
have turned away from me, and by their eyes, which have lust-
ed after idols. They will loath themselves for the evil they have
done and for all their detestable practices" (Ezekiel 6:9b).

It is so sad to see our wonderful United States of America,
which was founded on prayer and Scripture, disintegrate right
before our eyes. Many lives were lost in wars to protect our way
of life as laid out in the Constitution and Bill of Rights. Our

laws were previously based on God's Word. Our Pledge of Allegiance to our flag states, "one nation under God." Our nation has stood firm for well over 200 years under the favor of our God. But things have changed.

The moral and spiritual fiber of this nation has been corrupted little by little until many people do not even know what is right and what is wrong. There is so much deception through false and biased news reporting and the influence of movies, TV, and videos that are so filled with illicit behavior and violence that it influences attitudes and actions. Society has been desensitized to accept corruption as the norm. Add the consequences of drugs and alcohol to the mix, and it makes fertile ground for all kinds of crime, disrespect, and disobedience to authorities and parents. All this has been predicted in Scripture.

> But mark this: There will be terrible times in the last days. People will be lovers of themselves, lovers of money, boastful, proud, abusive, disobedient to their parents, ungrateful, unholy, without love, unforgiving, slanderous, without self-control, brutal, not lovers of the good, treacherous, rash, conceited, lovers of pleasure rather than lovers of God—having a form of godliness but denying its power. Have nothing to do with them. (2 Timothy 3:1–5)

Another area that is eroding our nation, as well as individuals, is dependence on the government. Welfare is a good thing for people who cannot be self-supportive through no fault of their own. Political correctness and over-the-top welfare to people who are possibly reaping the results of irresponsible behavior is making generations dependent on the government, which eventually takes away the drive for creativity, work ethic, self-reliance, etc. Reducing those virtues has harmed self-esteem, confidence, and pride in accomplishments. That pattern of dependence tears down self-worth, which can usher in jealousy of the folks who have prosperity because they work and enjoy these beneficial qualities.

These values have not been taught in many classrooms and homes. It can breed despair, hopelessness, and a mindset of dependence affecting generation after generation.

I heard a woman who called into a radio talk show. She said that she had been on welfare (and listed all her benefits) for over thirty years. Now her grown children are on it too. She asked why she would work since she gets everything that she needs with welfare benefits. The radio host asked her if she would work if she did not get welfare. She responded with yes. She also said that she was continuing to receive offers for more welfare benefits.

The reaction to the COVID-19 pandemic has raised our national debt as well as given the government more power and control. Much of these stimulus packages were spent on things that had nothing to do with the pandemic.

There are "now hiring" signs all over town. However, the large stimulus checks and increased unemployment checks facilitated many people who could work to choose not to work and depend on the government hand-outs. This undermines initiative and self-reliance that could strengthen them through this period. In the Great Depression, people took whatever job they could find. They did not expect the government to support them.

Who is paying these generous handouts? Not Uncle Sam. It is the taxpayers.

"If a man will not work, he shall not eat. We hear that some among you are idle. They are not busy; they are busybodies. Such people we command and urge in the Lord Jesus Christ to settle down and earn the bread they eat" (2 Thessalonians 3:10b–12).

Perhaps the pandemic has made people with large credit card debt wake up and realize that they really don't need everything that they had charged. People formerly saved for their purchases and bought them when they had the funds to pay for them. That is basically living within their means. We live in a generation that expects instant gratification in every area.

"The rich rule over the poor, and the borrower is slave to the lender" (Proverbs 22:7).

Many people need a helping hand to get back on track because of the pandemic. I am grateful for the help they received. But many others are content to let the taxpayers pay their way, even when there is no pandemic. This can also tear down the morale of the people who do work. Also, many businesses have had to close because of the shortage of workers.

It is right to do for others what they cannot do for themselves, but we should not do for people who are able but will not do for themselves. Most people can do some type of work.

"Make it your ambition to lead a quiet life, to mind your own business and to work with your hands, just as we told you, so that your daily life may win the respect of outsiders and so that you will not be dependent on anybody" (1 Thessalonians 4:11).

When a nation turns away from God, His judgement can be expected. However, His children hold on to hope because of God's promises.

"When I shut up the heavens so that there is no rain, or command locusts to devour the land or send a plague among my people, if my people who are called by name, will humble themselves and pray and seek my face and turn from their wicked ways, then will I hear from heaven and will forgive their sin and will heal their land" (2 Chronicles 7:13–14).

Notice it says, "seek My face." It seems that we are usually seeking His hand of provision and neglect seeking Him for who He is and for an intimate relationship with Him. Also, notice "and turn from their wicked ways." Ask God to show you, individually, your own wicked ways. Ask Him to open your eyes to see where you have been desensitized and turn around, letting go of the wicked ways. Ask the Lord, "Would You watch this with me or participate in this with me; is this honoring to You?" Nothing is done in secret from God. He is the lover of your very soul. "Nothing in all creation is hidden from God's sight. Everything is uncovered and laid bare before the eyes of him to whom we must give account" (Hebrews 4:13).

"Do not conform any longer to the pattern of this world, but be transformed by the renewing of your mind. Then you will be able to test and approve what God's will is—his good, pleasing, and perfect will" (Romans 12:2).

By hearing all the negative reports on social media and some news broadcasts, we can be led to believe that the number of Christians is extremely small. In 1 Kings 19:14, Elijah replied, "I have been very zealous for the LORD God Almighty. The Israelites have rejected your covenant, broken down your altars, put your prophets to death with the sword. I am the only one left, and now they are trying to kill me too."

But God had more plans for Elijah. He gave Elijah further assignments and told Elijah in verse 18, "Yet I reserve seven thousand in Israel—all whose knees have not bowed down to Baal and all whose mouths have not kissed him."

God still has His people. Although there are many who go to church and claim to be Christians, some are not. True Christians are the church, not a building or denomination.

There are those who have listened to the devil's lies and deceived themselves that their religion would save them.

It is as Jesus told Nicodemus in John 3:5–7, "I tell you the truth, no one can enter the kingdom of God unless he is born of water and the Spirit. Flesh gives birth to flesh, but the Spirit gives birth to spirit. You should not be surprised by my saying, 'You must be born again.'"

A man-made religion amounts to nothing, no matter how extravagant the rituals, no matter how many repetitious prayers are said. Jesus is the Savior. It is only by His blood shed on the cross that He saved us. He is the eternal Priest.

"For there is one God and one Mediator between God and men, the Man Christ Jesus, who gave Himself a ransom for all, to be testified in due time" (1 Timothy 2:5 NKJV).

"He is Lord of lords and King of kings" (Revelation 17:14b).

True Christians can be deceived when they become enamored with the things of this world. Examples are power, wealth, politics, careers, revering celebrities in sports, movie stars, hobbies, and so on. Satan uses these things to deceive us into making them the focus of life above God.

> When tempted, no one should say, 'God is tempting me.' For God cannot be tempted by evil, nor does he tempt anyone; but each one is tempted when, by his own evil desire, he is dragged away and enticed. Then, after desire has conceived, it gives birth to sin, and sin, when it is full-grown, gives birth to death. (James 1:13–15)

Bible prophecy has always been fulfilled. Much of the Bible has been proven through archeology and history already. There is yet more prophecy to be fulfilled. There are prophecies throughout the Bible in reference to the last days.

I challenge you to read the book of Revelation. "Blessed is the one who reads the words of this prophecy, and blessed are those who hear it and take it to heart what is written in it, because the time is near" (Revelation 1:3).

Look around this whole world; it is ripe for judgement. In Revelation, Jesus has letters for the churches containing commendation and correction. There are many warnings of the tribulation and wrath to come for those who have not received Jesus.

> But because of your stubbornness and your unrepentant heart, you are storing up wrath against yourself for the day of God's wrath, when his righteous judgement will be revealed. God "will give to each person according to what he has done." To those who by persistence in doing good seek glory, honor, and immortality, he will give eternal life. But for those who are self-seeking and who reject the truth and follow evil, there will be wrath and anger. (Romans 2:5–8)

There are also promises and prophecies for those who are in Christ because they have believed and received Jesus, the Son of God, as their Savior and Lord.

"They will see the Son of Man coming on the clouds of the sky, with power and great glory. And he will send his angels with a loud trumpet call, and they will gather his elect from the four winds, from one end of the heavens to the other" (Matthew 24:30b–31).

> No one knows about that day or hour, not even the angels in heaven, nor the Son, but only the Father. As it was in the days of Noah, so it will be at the coming of the Son of Man. For in the days before the flood, people were eating and drinking, marrying, and giving in marriage, up to the day Noah entered the ark; and they knew nothing about what would happen until the flood came and took them all away. (Matthew 24:36–39)

When Jesus returns to take up the church in the rapture, there will not be a flood this time. Great tribulation and the wrath of God will follow, as described in the book of Revelation. Jesus, Himself describes this even more in Matthew 24 and 25.

To me, it seems that all things are lining up for Jesus to come again soon. In one day, Israel became a nation again on May 14, 1948, after about 2000 years.

"Who has heard such a thing? Who has seen such things? Shall a land be born in one day? Or shall a nation be brought forth in a moment? For as soon as Zion was in labor, she brought forth her children" (Isaiah 66:8 AMP).

"Truly, I tell you, this generation (that is, those living at that definite period of time), will not perish and pass away until all has taken place" (Luke 21:32 AMP).

Luke 21 gives a lot of description about the last days.

> But take heed to yourselves and be on your guard lest your hearts be overburdened and depressed—weighted down—with the giddiness and headache and nausea of self-indulgence, drunkenness, and worldly worries and cares pertaining to (the business of) this life, and that day come upon you suddenly like a trap or a noose; for it will come upon all who live upon the face of the entire earth. (Luke 21:34–35 AMP)

Scriptures tell us that deceivers will claim that they are Christ. Luke 21:8 states, "Watch out that you are not deceived. For many will come in my name, claiming, 'I am He.'" I have heard of claims like that in my own lifetime.

In Revelation, it describes the one-world government led by the Antichrist. Many of our own government leaders are drawing us closer to a one-world government.

The time is now to stop being deceived by the rhetoric that is all around us, which is designed to convince us to compromise the Word of God and embrace the lies of Satan.

It is time to turn to God in repentance and receive Christ or turn back to Him. This world is a temporary place for all of us. The pandemic has drawn attention to the fact that any of us can die at any time. We basically are all terminal unless we are in the multitude that is taken up in the rapture when Jesus returns.

The Bible was written by men inspired by God over thousands of years. It is still totally relevant today.

Don't let the current culture and worldview lead you astray. Eternity is reality. Heaven or hell is forever. The only way to heaven is through faith in Jesus Christ.

"Whoever believes in him is not condemned, but whoever does not believe stands condemned already because he has not believed in the name of God's one and only [begotten] Son" (John 3:18).

> My dear brothers, take note of this: Everyone should be quick to listen, slow to speak and slow to become angry, for man's anger does not bring about the righteous life that God desires. Therefore, get rid of all moral filth and the evil that is so prevalent and humbly accept the word planted in you, which can save you. Do not merely listen to the word, and so deceive yourselves. Do what it says. (James 1:19–22)

Although the door to the future does not have a doorknob, God has revealed, within Scripture, what the future holds for those who believe in Jesus, the Son of God. Also, for those who have not received Him as their Savior and Lord.

Get off the fence, stop compromising, and give yourself

to Him! His love and care will get you through anything, and His Holy Spirit will come and live in you. You can give all your burdens to Him. You will never be alone, and His promises will apply to you.

Chapter 16
Cross in the Tiles

As you look closely at the tiles on the floor of the hallway in the painting, you will see the cross. That is our foundation for every day. It is the hope we have because of the cross and the empty grave. Jesus Christ died for our sins. He took them upon Himself, was buried, then He rose from the dead. That is what baptism represents. When we receive Jesus as our Savior and Lord and are baptized, we identify with His death, burial, and resurrection. We are dead to our old self and are now alive in Christ. His sacrifice has reconciled us to God, our heavenly Father.

Each day we have the cross as a reminder to take up our own cross by taking off our old self of flesh and walking in the Spirit. "So I say, live by the Spirit, and you will not gratify the desires of the sinful nature" (Galatians 5:16). "There is therefore now no condemnation for those who are in Christ Jesus, who do not walk according to the flesh, but according to the Spirit" (Romans 8:1 NKJV).

Scripture explains that we take communion in remembrance of Him.

> The Lord Jesus on the same night in which He was betrayed took bread; and when He had given thanks, He broke it and said, "Take eat; this is My body which is broken for you; do this in remembrance of Me." In the same manner He also took the cup after supper, saying, "This cup is the new covenant in My blood. This do, as often as you drink it, in remembrance of Me." For as often as you eat this bread and drink this cup, you proclaim the Lord's death till He comes. (1 Corinthians 11:23b–26 NKJV)

The cross in the tiles reminds us of the sovereignty of God. He is the Creator and Master of the universe, yet He knows how many hairs are on our heads. His greatness is more than we can fathom. Think about the cells in our bodies, plants, trees, animals, everything. Think of the fullness of the seas and the earth. He knows each one of us individually and loves us beyond measure. His thoughts are beyond ours. He is not constrained by time.

"Be still and know that I am God" (Psalm 46:10a).

He reveals Himself in nature and in Scripture. When we draw near Him, He will draw near to us. Even when we don't seek Him, He seeks us. He desires intimate fellowship with each of us so much that He convicts us when we go astray. "Those whom I love I rebuke and discipline. So be earnest, and repent. Here I am! I stand at the door and knock. If anyone hears my voice and opens the door, I will come in and eat with him, and he with me" (Revelation 3:19–20).

The awesome, one and only true God wants fellowship with each of us! He wants to dialogue with us. Prayer is talking to Him and listening to what He says in our minds and spirit as well as through Scripture. Be alert throughout your day to decern His presence.

We can call on His names. There are many listed in Scripture. Here are some of them:

Lord God Most High, God in Heaven, Prince of Peace, The Lord Will Provide, The Holy God, The Lord of Hosts, The God Who Forgives, The God Who Sees Me, The God of My Strength, Everlasting God, The Faithful God, The Living God, The Lord Your Savior, Master Over All, The God Who Is Near, God with Us, The Lord Our Healer.

We can rest in His love and enjoy communication with God Almighty! "You will keep him in perfect peace, whose mind is stayed on You, because he trusts in You" (Isaiah 26:3 NKJV).

Rest; that inner peace and stillness come when we trust God enough to let go of our control and allow God to have full reign in our lives and the lives of others. Jesus would go away to a private place to pray to the heavenly Father. When He ministered and preached to the crowds, He passed on to them what the Father had told Him to say and do. He submitted fully to His Father's will. If God's Son depended on the Father, who are we to try to manage on our own?

It is in our nature to want to be in control of every aspect of our lives as well as being inclined to hover over other people to make sure they are doing things as we think they should be done. Plus, we think if we don't take care of it, who will? This, of course, causes a lot of stress which can result in all kinds of negative ramifications.

The cross in the tiles reminds us that our God gives us the privilege to relinquish everything to His control. He is Lord of all! He wants us to approach Him like little children and depend on Him as our heavenly Father. We try so hard to be strong in our own strength. However, we have access to the Lord for strength, courage, guidance, and anything we need.

The more time we spend with Him, the more we get to know Him and love Him. It is amazing that He wants to have an intimate relationship with each of us. Some things are just too enormous for us to grasp in our finite beings. It is such a privilege to have fellowship with our God. We walk away from our personal time with Him, blessed and refreshed.

A common excuse is, "I don't have time to have a quiet time with the Lord." We live in an age of information overload. Some things can be eliminated or reduced from our frantic pace. Take time to analyze your schedule. Your quiet time, basking in His love, will surely help your body and mind relax and realign to meet the challenges you face each day. Remember about sending the upsetting things of the past through the slot in the Past/Yesterday door. We can't go through the Tomorrow/Future door. However, we can trust the Lord with our tomorrow. We can send up those worry balloons with prayer and praise, letting them go to the Lord. Ask the Holy Spirit to show you what you can release in order to have special personal time with God.

I have read that in the 1700s, Susannah Wesley, from England, was the mother of Charles and John Wesley, who became worldwide Christian leaders. I have also read that she had a total of nineteen children, although not all survived. In order to have quiet time with the Lord, she would flip her apron over her head to cover her face. I assume that her children knew not to interrupt her while she was praying. If there is a desire to meet with God, there is surely a way.

> As the Father has loved me, so have I loved you. Now remain in my love. If you obey my commands, you will remain in my love, just as I have obeyed my Father's commands and remain in his love. I have told you this so that my joy may be in you and that your joy may be complete. My command is this: Love each other as I have loved you. (John 15:9–11)

Do you see how important the cross in the tiles is for our Today? I will never understand how people survive without a personal union with Christ. Any time in our day, we can look on the cross and be reassured and strengthened that our God has everything in His hands, even if the circumstances seem impossible to overcome. He is working out His plans, and we get to be a part. We, as Christians, have our heavenly home to look forward to with Him. That thought makes the troubles of any moment fade in comparison to the wonders ahead for us.

As we let go of ourselves, we don't have to be self-defensive since we have already surrendered ourselves and our possessions to God. "But I tell you, Love your enemies and pray for those who persecute you, to show that you are the children of your Father Who is in heaven" (Matthew 5:44–45a AMP). Ignore petty insults or hurt feelings. Don't retaliate. Maintain your composure and self-respect.

That does not mean to be a doormat, but the importance of making a point or clinging to a possession is not significant anymore. How much more relaxed our days would be if we could keep in mind that we are just traveling through. This is not our home.

The cross and all it represents is the central point of the painting. It is the pivotal point for all humanity.

Chapter 17

Abiding in Christ

In the garden of Gethsemane, just before His arrest, Jesus was praying for His disciples and us. "My prayer is not for them alone. I pray also for those who will believe in me through their message, that all of them may be one, Father, just as you are in me and I am in you. May they also be in us so that the world may believe that you have sent me" (John 17:20–21).

Jesus told His disciples about the Holy Spirit, who would come to them after He was gone to be with the heavenly Father.

> "If you love me, you will obey what I command. And I will ask the Father, and he will give you another Counselor to be with you forever—the Spirit of truth. The world cannot accept him, because it neither sees him nor knows him. But you know him, for he lives with you and will be in you" (John 14:15–17).

"He who loves me will be loved by my Father, and I too will love him and show myself to him" (John 14:21b).

It is so wonderful that Jesus does show Himself to us through the Holy Spirit who lives in believers. He gives us understanding of the Scriptures, guides us, and gives us discernment. As we depend on Him each day, He comforts us and reminds us of everything that He has taught us. He blesses us so richly as we stay in Him. "I am the vine; you are the branches. If a man remains in me and I in him, he will bear much fruit; apart from me you can do nothing" (John 15:5).

Another part of Jesus' prayer in the garden was asking the Father to take the cup from Him. He knew the suffering that was for Him to experience. Then He said, "Yet not what I will, but what You will" (Mark 14:36b).

"Not everyone who says to me, 'Lord, Lord,' will enter the kingdom of heaven, but only he who does the will of my Father" (Matthew 7:21).

We each are prompted by the Holy Spirit to do or say things that benefit others. God has chosen to allow us to participate in His plans. What a blessing!

"Anyone, then, who knows the good he ought to do and doesn't do it, sins" (James 4:17).

We must humbly submit; then be alert and watch how He works during your day. It is awesome to begin a new day being submitted to God's will.

One day, I was coming out of the grocery store when I passed a young man, an employee of the store, taking his break just sitting in his car with loud music playing. The Lord prompted me to go back and tell him that Jesus loves him. I did obey, then walked back to my car. Then the young man came over to me, thanked me, and told me that he needed to hear that message at that specific time. It is such a privilege when the Lord allows us to participate with Him in ministering to others.

Another time, I was in a restaurant when I spotted a woman who was, obviously to me, experiencing sorrow and stress. I went over to her and asked her if I could pray for her. She said yes. I did not ask her what her problem was. I just depended on the Lord to guide my prayer. It is a humbling feeling to be allowed to be involved in God's purposes. He will use you, too, as you stay in tune with Him. Listen for Him to speak to you with promptings in your spirit. Step out and obey. What joy!

The Holy Spirit lives the life of Christ through us. We cannot force the Spirit to work through us by our own effort. As we rely on Him in complete surrender, He uses us for God's glory.

Isn't that what it is all about? We want to glorify God as we live, move, and have our being in Jesus.

Anxiously trying to be good enough for God can never be achieved. We always fall short. He knows that we are human beings. Since we can never measure up to His holiness, He offers us the righteousness and holiness of Christ in order to be reconciled to the Father. We cannot wrap our human minds around that fact. Some things require to be understood in the spirit as we abide in Christ.

As we trust Jesus with all our hearts, we are giving Him complete control over every aspect of our lives. He knows our thoughts, our hearts, and all the segments of our situations. We need Him constantly to lead us in every circumstance. But He will not interfere if we insist on our own wisdom. He wants us to consult Him and ask for guidance.

The cross in the tiles can be a reminder to surrender people to Him that we have tried to help, but our efforts never brought about any change that would turn them from their bondage to an abundant life in Christ. They just are not receptive. Until they are ready to take responsibility for their own life, they cannot be helped in a long-term way. Unless they are ready to stop making excuses and disconnect from people who influence their behavior negatively, coaching and bailing them out of their messes is not going to resolve their dysfunctional lives. Face it; you are not supposed to be their savior. Some people are running from God! Do you want to support them in that effort?

The door is always open for Jesus to forgive them if they come to Him with a heart of repentance. Let the cross in the tiles be a daily reminder to you to get out of the way and allow God to rescue them in His way and timing.

Our prayers must always be God-centered, not self-centered, no matter if it is for your needs, confession of sins, interceding for someone, or seeking guidance and His will.

The cross also reminds us to get our priorities in order and remove distractions that are taking our focus away from trust in the Lord. He knows what we need, but sometimes our lives can become so cluttered that we have difficulty decerning what really is necessary, what is truly important.

"But seek first his kingdom and his righteous, and all these things will be given to you as well" (Matthew 6:33).

It is a matter of deliberately pursuing living in His kingdom here on earth and walking in surrender to Him. What are your priorities? Do you choose to give Him first place in every part of your life? As we walk in obedience to Him, He takes care of our needs.

When we are weary of waiting for prayer to be answered, the cross in the tiles assures us that God is sovereign and has everything in His control. His timing is always the right timing. Regrets surely follow getting ahead of God. Trust Him. The answer to some prayers may not come until we are already gone from this world.

While we are waiting, we are to be going forward with whatever He has for us to be doing right now. He does not need our supervision or intervention. I always need to remember that He is God; I am not!

Chapter 18

Music Notes

The music notes in the sky represent our praise, worship, prayers, and thanksgiving. Oh, the joy of praising our God. He is worthy, so worthy! "I will sing to the LORD all my life; I will sing praise to my God as long as I live" (Psalm 104:33).

Years ago, I was a part of a very large congregation in Phoenix, Arizona. When we were all singing praises along with the choir, it felt as if we were standing before the throne of God on holy ground. It is so wonderful to have time especially set aside to corporately express our acknowledgement, appreciation, and adoration to God.

It is also a joy to spontaneously break into songs of praise at home. Can't sing? Scripture says, "Make a joyful noise to the Lord, all you lands!" (Psalm 100:1 AMP). It is amazing how praise and worship can change our attitude as we focus on the Lord instead of our problems. We are lifted above the storms of life to a place of peace as we gain the perspective of eternity instead of the world.

"Oh, give thanks to the LORD! Call upon His name; Make known His deeds among the peoples! Sing to Him, sing psalms to Him; Talk of all His wondrous works!" (Psalm 105:1–2 NKJV).

As well as singing, we can worship our Lord in our daily lives by the way we live in obedience to His commands. We can worship Him by the way we treat other people. "Religion that God our Father accepts as pure and faultless is this: to look after orphans and widows in their distress and to keep oneself from being polluted by the world" (James 1:27). When you send up prayers, remember to pray with thanksgiving. We are so earthly-minded that our prayers are, many times, like a shopping list of things that apply to our current circumstances. The Father already knows our needs and wants us to seek His wisdom, provision, and intervention. But above all that, He wants personal communion with us.

Do you pause to reflect on His goodness and His love for you? He desires that we seek His face, seek to know Him on a deeper level. Do you take time to focus on gratitude for all He has already done for you? Or do you treat Him like a Santa in the sky? It is the intangibles that bring us peace and joy in this special relationship with our Holy God. How often do you think about who He is and thank Him for the Holy Spirit's sanctifying work in you, changing you on the inside to reflect Christ in you?

I was just thinking about the famous painting of Jesus standing at the door and knocking. That door does not have a doorknob. It is up to the person inside to open the door and invite Him in. He so desires to have a personal, intimate relationship with each of us. It is incredible that the God of the universe loves each individual person so much. This is more than we can grasp in our human minds.

I know we are earthly beings, but we are also spiritual beings. "For though we live in the world, we do not wage war as the world does. The weapons we fight with are not the weapons of the world. On the contrary, they have divine power to demolish strongholds" (2 Corinthians 10:3–4).

"Refute arguments and theories and reasonings and every proud and lofty thing that sets itself up against true knowledge of God; and we lead every thought and purpose away captive into the obedience of Christ, the Messiah, the Anointed One" (2 Corinthians 10:5 AMP).

That is why we must stay in constant connection to our Lord in prayer. We face choices every day, and we need the spiritual power to combat the temptations of the flesh and the deceptions of Satan.

> This is how you can recognize the Spirit of God: Every spirit that acknowledges that Jesus Christ has come in the flesh is from God, but every spirit that does not acknowledge Jesus is not from God. This is the spirit of the antichrist, which you have heard is coming and even now is already in the world. You, dear children, are from God and have overcome them, because the one who is in you is greater than the one who is in the world. (1 John 4:2–4)

It is the power of the Holy Spirit within us that gives us the strength and power to overcome the flesh. As we take in nourishment from the Scriptures and the transforming work of the Holy Spirit, we grow in Christ. We are so privileged to go directly to the throne room of our heavenly Father with our praise and requests. Jesus made that possible by the cross.

As we meditate on the greatness of our God and the promises that He has given us, we can't help but think how very unworthy we are to be in the position He has placed us in the heavenly realm.

> As for you, you were dead in your transgressions and sins, in which you used to live when you followed the ways of this world and of the ruler of the kingdom of the air [Satan], the spirit who is now at work in those who are disobedient. All of us also lived among them at one time, gratifying the cravings of our sinful nature and following its desires and thoughts. Like the rest, we were by nature objects of wrath. But because of his great love for us, God, who is rich in mercy, made us alive with Christ even when we were dead in trans-

gressions—it is by grace you have been saved. And God raised us up with Christ and seated us with him in the heavenly realms in Christ Jesus, in order that in the coming ages he might show the incomparable riches of his grace, expressed in his kindness to us in Christ Jesus. For it is by grace you have been saved, through faith—and this not from yourselves, it is the gift of God—not by works, so that no one can boast. For we are God's workmanship, created in Christ Jesus to do good works, which God prepared in advance for us to do. (Ephesians 2:1–10)

He is so worthy of our continuous worship, obedience, honor, and praise. The focus can be shifted from our earthly concerns to His desires and His glory. We want to align our prayers with His will. Do we stop and ask our heavenly Father what He wants us to pray about?

"Be joyful always, pray continually, give thanks in all circumstances, for this is God's will for you in Christ Jesus" (1 Thessalonians 5:16–18).

Chapter 19
Gratitude

Where do we begin as we count our blessings? We can fill the sky with music notes of thanksgiving every day as we think about the awesomeness of our God. We are profusely blessed in every way, especially in this nation of the United States of America, the land of opportunity. We are so privileged to be citizens of a nation that was founded on God's principles, Scripture, and prayer. We pray that this foundation will be preserved.

People all over the world are blessed with the opportunity to seek and find our Creator.

"For since the creation of the world God's invisible qualities—his eternal power and divine nature—have been clearly seen, being understood from what has been made, so that men are without excuse" (Romans 1:20).

He has given us such beauty in nature. His wonders are always before our eyes. His artistry is displayed in the dawn and evening sky. The stars proclaim His majesty and the magnitude of Himself. He has given us our senses to enjoy His handiwork. Each of us is a masterpiece of His creation. When we stop and meditate on all He has created for us, we can overflow with gratitude for all the tangible things He has given us to enjoy. We want to send up our music notes of praise and thanksgiving.

The spiritual blessings that He has given to us are forever into eternity, for which we give lavish praise and thanksgiving to Him. He gave us His Son, the greatest Gift. He provided the way for us to be reconciled to Him because we all were hopelessly separated from Him by our sins. God gives us His Holy Spirit to be in us while we are on this earth and seals us for eternity.

As we meditate on those glorious thoughts, it helps us get our perspective and priorities in order. How can we be so engrossed in the worldly indulgences and worries that occupy our thoughts and actions? As we transfer our thoughts to thanksgiving for the greatness of our sovereign God and who we are as His children, the things of this world fade in comparison.

> His divine power has given us everything we need for life and godliness through our knowledge of him who called us by his own glory and goodness. Through these he has given us his very great and precious promises, so that through them you may participate in the divine nature and escape the corruption in the world caused by evil desires. (2 Peter 1:3–4)

Since we have received Jesus as our Savior and the gift of the Holy Spirit, we have the power to resist doing wrong and embrace godliness as we grow in our new nature.

The Bible is filled with His promises to us and gives demonstrations of His goodness to His people. As His children, we can lay hold of these promises in our own lives as we joyously send our music notes of thanksgiving to the Lord. We are forever grateful for who He is as well as His wonderful attributes and promises. Reading Scripture will help you get to know our God better as your relationship with Him grows sweeter and more real to you as the days go by. A grateful attitude can even set the mood for your day.

"Be joyful always; pray continually; give thanks in all circumstances, for this is God's will for you in Christ Jesus" (1 Thessalonians 5:16–18).

Each day is a gift from God. We call it the present.

Chapter 20
Evening and Morning

"Those living far away fear your wonders; where morning dawns and evening fades you call forth songs of joy" (Psalm 65:8).

"Today Slips Away"

The Lord paints the evening skies with glorious colors of light
that change each moment until eventually fading into darkness.
A restful breeze ushers in the quietness.
A calmness comes as the stars begin to shine
and the moon glows above.
Joy fills our hearts as we contemplate our gracious God,
who has given all this for us to enjoy.
(Lynn Bryant)

"I lie down and sleep; I wake again, because the LORD sustains me" (Psalm 3:5).

"By day the LORD directs His love, at night His song is with me—a prayer to the God of my life" (Psalm 42:8).

"I will lie down and sleep in peace, for you alone, O LORD, make me dwell in safety" (Psalm 4:8).

"If you make the Most High your dwelling—even the LORD, who is my refuge—then no harm will befall you, no disaster will come near your tent" (Psalm 91:9–10).

"Another Today"

When each Today fades into the past
and the next day appears from the future,
we proceed in the present that God gives us.
Touches of morning fill the sky
with glimpses of glory in the brilliant sunrise.
We lift our voices in joyful praise
as we welcome the dawn of a fresh new Today.
(Lynn Bryant)

What is that sound, the alarm clock already? Are you tempted to hit the snooze button? Be brave, take authority, and gently pull yourself up out of that bed. Put your feet on the floor, and make up the bed before you give in to temptation and crawl back under the covers. Give voice to the proclamation, "This is the day that the Lord has made; let us [I will] rejoice and be glad in it" (Psalm 118:24) [my personalization]. Boldly make that decision.

Even if you are temporarily going forward on auto-pilot, you know the way to the bathroom. When you see yourself in the mirror, instead of counting the wrinkles, just laugh! Then, on to the coffee pot, if you like. By now, you are awake enough to get your Bible, go to your quiet space, and spend some precious time with the Lover of your soul.

Each person establishes their own routine that works for them, even if it means getting up earlier. It can be hard to find the time for our special meeting with the Lord; however, we can choose to make it a priority and do it or not. You will certainly be rewarded for your efforts.

The book of Proverbs is a good place to explore. It is so full of practical wisdom that applies today as much as when they were written.

I often pray using Scripture as my guide. The following verse is one of my favorites.

"Roll your works upon the Lord—commit and trust them wholly to Him; [He will cause your thoughts to become agreeable to His will, and] so shall your plans be established and succeed" (Proverbs 16:3 AMP).

My prayer paraphrase is, "Dear Lord, I commit my works into Your hands, please establish my plans, cause them to succeed, and even my thoughts to be in conformity to Yours."

Jesus will reveal Himself to you through Scripture and speak to you by the Holy Spirit with a knowing, or prompting, or even through different circumstances. He is not limited in how He communicates to you. But pray for discernment, and don't be deceived by other voices. He will never contradict Scripture.

"Whoever has my commands and obeys them, he is the one who loves me. He who loves me will be loved by my Father, and I too will love him and show myself to him" (John 14:21).

The elements of the painting may be helpful during your time of prayer. Remember to begin with the music notes of thanksgiving, praise, and adoration.

As you are praying, bring your worries, burdens, and concerns to the Lord. Then release those yellow balloons as you turn them over to Him.

Ask Him what and whom He wants you to pray about. Seek His heart.

In case there are some past issues to discuss and sins to confess, pray about them; then slide them through the slot in the Past/Yesterday door. Leave them behind. Listen to the Lord's instructions if He wants you to take any actions regarding them. Forgive everyone for any wrongs against you. Reconcile with those with whom you have offended.

Plan and act upon any matters that He directs for today, tomorrow, or the future. Go ahead, plant seeds for flowers and spiritual seeds into people's lives. Just remember that only Today is what you have, so make wise choices and decisions as you consult our heavenly Father.

"In the morning, O LORD, you hear my voice; in the morning I lay my requests before you and wait in expectation" (Psalm 5:3).

Some of my recurring prayers for my grown children are filed in the "hope and wait" category as they have been for years. But I still expect my heavenly Father to fulfill my hope in His timing and His way. I repeatedly replace my grief with hope and trust in the Lord as I continue to commit them to Him. I thank God that I am no longer paralyzed, spending my life trying to rescue my children from their life situations so that they could live peaceful, happy lives walking with the Lord. My expectations for them only led to disappointment. It took a very long time for me to realize that it was not in my capability to bring positive changes in them. God will work out His plans in their lives, even if I have already passed away from this world. That is between them and the Lord. That is His business, not mine. As a result of that realization, I am determined to go forward with assured hope and trust in God. I will not waste my Todays; instead, I will pursue the Lord's purposes that He wants to accomplish through me.

I pray the following Scripture prayer for you and myself:

"May the God of hope fill you with all joy and peace as you trust in him, so that you may overflow with hope by the power of the Holy Spirit" (Romans 15:13).

Throughout each day, I try to keep my mind on the cross in the tiles, which reminds me of God's sovereignty. He has everything under control, so I can walk in peace and freedom as I keep sending up those music notes of thanksgiving and praise to the One who watchfully cares for us. His unconditional love for you is greater than anyone on this earth can love you.

In the Psalms, we are reminded over and over that "His steadfast love endures forever." "How great is the love the Father has lavished on us, that we should be called children of God! And that is what we are!" (1 John 3:1a).

A daily habit for me is to reestablish in my mind that God is God; I am not. It takes a great burden off me as I can release anxiety and stress to Him and surrender myself to Him.

This takes daily practice to consciously choose to consult and submit to Him in every situation that arises throughout the day. I pray for the Holy Spirit to guard my mouth and alert me before I plunge in and try to handle things my own way.

I wish so much that I had been more receptive to practically applying Scripture much earlier in my life. I think a big problem for many of us is that there seems to be so much stuff going on all the time. We are too busy and preoccupied to hear and apply God's instructions and allow the Holy Spirit to speak to us. We must take time to analyze and rearrange our priorities.

We are so accustomed to living in this world and attending to the things of this world that we neglect seeking first His kingdom and His righteousness.

This morning in my quiet time, it came to me about the meaning of a phrase that is repeated several times in the New Testament: "He who has an ear, let him hear." Those seeking God are attentive to hear. They are granted spiritual understanding. They accept what is revealed to them (Matthew 11:15, 13:9, 43; Mark 4:23; Luke 14:35; Revelation 2:7).

Some people just do not want to hear. They close their ears and won't listen to anyone. If people are not receptive, they cannot understand what He is teaching. They are not willing to acknowledge their need to surrender to God where they could find rest. We can pray for the healing of spiritually deaf ears as well as hearts to be open to be able to receive all He wants to reveal.

We all have had a problem with Godship, living as if we are Holy Spirit junior. What a shame. Our Lord has suffered so much to provide wonderful benefits to us, His children, yet we spurn His ways and follow our own ways and understanding.

"Trust in the LORD with all your heart and lean not on your own understanding; in all your ways acknowledge him and he will make your paths straight. Do not be wise in your own eyes; fear the LORD and shun evil" (Proverbs 3:5–7).

Our Father is so patient as the Holy Spirit works to sanctify us throughout our lives, conforming us to the image of His Son.

As we acquire an eternal perspective, we won't be so likely to be derailed by trivial distractions or give in to discouragement as pain and trials come along. As we allow our dear Lord to direct our choices and decisions, we can rest in Him and serve in His kingdom here on earth, all the while looking forward to living in His heavenly kingdom.

A powerful way of staying on course in your quiet time with the Lord is to have a journal to record your thoughts, prayers, His answers, and directions, as well as insights and applications that He reveals to you about Scripture. You may even want to write down Scriptures that are special to you or apply to whatever you are praying about. You can refer to your notes later.

I learned about journaling many years ago when I lived in Grand Junction, Colorado. It brought me to a closer communication with the Lord. Some of my entries are prayers written just like a personal letter to my heavenly Father. It is full of Scriptures that gave me guidance in different situations.

One time when I was praying and asking God to look in my heart and tell me what He saw, immediately the answer dropped into my mind, "Forgiven." It brought tears of humility and gratitude to my eyes. It was not about any certain sin. It was like a covering over my heart.

It is so sweet when we spend focused undisturbed time with our Lord. It brings a closeness that I cannot describe. There is a knowing of His presence that is so precious. There is no earthly comparison. It makes me think of being a little child cuddled up in my heavenly Father's lap, safe and secure.

I love You, my Lord! There go those melody notes up into the sky. To be enveloped in His love transcends anything this world has to offer. It feels as if I am standing on the threshold of a fresh beginning in my life. The things the Lord has revealed to me while writing this book have brought me into a deeper understanding of His kingdom perspective. I feel as if He is preparing us for what is ahead as He carries out His plans for the future.

"Forget the former things; do not dwell on the past. See, I am doing a new thing! Now it springs up; do you not perceive it? I am making a way in the desert and streams in the wasteland" (Isaiah 43:18–19).

It is imperative that we let go of the irrelevant petty junk in our lives as well as let go of this world's enticements. It makes me think of an old hymn that talked about turning from this vain world's golden store and from each idol that says to Christians, "Love me more." The pandemic helped me to realize how much emphasis our culture puts on fulfilling self-indulgence and instant gratification. God promises to supply our needs, and the Bible warns against debt. As a nation, we are so materialistic and worldly-focused. It has crept in upon most of us. People, we need to wake up! Jesus tells us that He will return like a thief in the night, a time when people don't expect Him. Will you be ready? Are you longing and looking for Him to return? Remember, this world is temporary. You can't wait until you see Him coming in the clouds to take up the believers and then cry out. It will happen instantly.

Jesus Himself said to His disciples, "Go into all the world and preach the good news to all creation. Whoever believes and is baptized will be saved, but whoever does not believe will be condemned" (Mark 16:15–16).

The downfall of many nations, as recorded in Scripture and history, was because of their worship of idols instead of the only true God. Some worshiped both God and idols. "They made him jealous with their foreign gods and angered him with their detestable idols" (Deuteronomy 32:16). You can read verses 17–38 to learn of the terrible consequences of this behavior.

"See now that I myself am He! There is no god besides me" (Deuteronomy 32:39a).

"You shall have no other gods before me" (Exodus 20:3).

I wonder if we, as believers, are holding onto idols, things we prioritize over our relationship with God, our Creator. Since we have received Jesus as our Savior, we must accept Him as Lord over our whole lives, abandon our old nature, and put on our new selves. Walk in the Spirit, not in the flesh. Scripture defines both in Galatians 6:19–24.

The first commandment is "Love the Lord your God with all your heart and with all your soul and with all your mind and with all your strength" (Mark 12:30). He deserves all our love and allegiance. Think of all He has done for us to reconcile us, adopt us as His children, and give us eternal life! He will not share His throne with any other gods. We each will give account of ourselves before Him.

"But you, brothers, are not in darkness so that this day should surprise you like a thief. For God did not appoint us to suffer wrath but to receive salvation through our Lord Jesus Christ" (1 Thessalonians 5:4, 9).

O dear God, thank You that You are transforming us into the image of Christ, to love You as You deserve to be loved. Help us to live our lives being a pleasure to You. Continue to teach us to let go of all that distracts us from total devotion to You. Give us discernment to know what really matters in your perspective. Thank You, in Jesus' name.

All people are born with a sinful nature since the fall of Adam and are under condemnation and deserving of God's wrath. But in our heavenly Father's marvelous plan, He provided the way for us to be reborn into a new creature. The old passes away, and we are new in Christ because Jesus died for our sins. He took the wrath of God upon Himself that was due to us. God gives us rebirth when we receive Jesus as our Savior and Lord.

"Therefore, there is now no condemnation for those who are in Christ Jesus, because through Christ Jesus the law of the Spirit of life set me free from the law of sin and death" (Romans 8:1–2).

Romans chapter 8 explains all this. God's incredible plan provides the way for us to be reconciled to Him. Once we receive Christ, we choose to spend the remainder of our lives willing to reject the dictates of the sinful nature and live controlled by the Spirit. It is a daily challenge, a daily surrender to our heavenly Father. We are faced every day with choices to live according to the flesh or the Spirit. When we are born again, God gives us the ability to live by the Spirit. As I meditate on all this, I am filled with gratitude for our God's miraculous provision to save us. How He loves us! He gives us the privilege to be His children and promises never to leave us or forsake us. We have an eternal future with Him.

> For the Lord himself will come down from heaven, with a loud command, with the voice of the archangel and with the trumpet call of God, and the dead in Christ will rise first. After that, we who are still alive and are

left will be caught up together with them in the clouds to meet the Lord in the air. And so, we will be with the Lord forever. (1 Thessalonians 4:16–17)

What a glorious day that will be. Praise His name forever! Come, Lord Jesus!

If your mind and environment are full of distractions that clutter your life, the less room you will have for Him to fill your life with His blessings of knowing Him in a personal, fulfilling relationship. When He is your priority, then life on this earth is an incredible journey. As we walk in His ways, we can have balance, peace, and joy. We can be a pleasure to Him as we submit to His will and bring honor to Him as He conforms us to the image of Christ.

Sometimes, in daily devotions, the Scripture verses that you are reading may seem to jump off the page into your mind. You want it to penetrate your heart so that you can meditate on it, act on it, and have it when you need to apply it later. It is amazing how the Holy Spirit will recall it for you when you need it in a later situation. You may want to write it down in your journal and express how it relates to you.

"But the Counselor, the Holy Spirit, whom the Father will send in my name, will teach you all things and will remind you of everything I have said to you" (John 14:26).

Chapter 21

Pages of Days

Today can be a beginning for you with our Lord as you participate in this journey by writing down your thoughts, notes, Scriptures, prayers, answers to prayer, etc. As you pray, listen, and absorb Scripture, your closeness with the Lord will grow. Many of you who are reading this book are already in personal communication with our Lord and know the joy and fulfillment it brings.

For the folks who would like some suggestions to get started on this daily walk, the following guidelines are based on the principles in Scripture that the painting represents.

Acknowledge our Sovereign God, as the cross in the tiles reminds us to declare Him as the only true Living God. Remember that Jesus purchased our salvation on the cross. Confirm in your heart His lordship over all creation as well as His involvement in your daily life.

Let your praise, worship, and adoration drift up to our heavenly Father like music notes in the air as you begin your new Today. You can become closer to God as you read about Him in the Psalms, which are filled with descriptions of His wonderful attributes and goodwill toward us. The Psalms also lead us in thanksgiving as we read and think about the benefits of being His children. In the Bible, we can discover how He lavishes His love and continuous blessings on us, which sustain us throughout our lives.

Confess sins and repent. Choose to turn away from those sins as you take one day at a time. Forgive others who have sinned against you. Then, stuff all that into the Past/Yesterday door slot with prayer and thanksgiving.

Present your specific requests to our heavenly Father with confidence that He hears and assurance that He will answer in His way and His timing.

Let go of worries and anxieties as you relinquish them to our heavenly Father with thanksgiving, and release those balloons into His care.

Surrender yourself to God and commit to be receptive and follow His instructions to you. Let your faith in Christ be evident by the way you live, by your good works and attitudes. This does not mean that you load yourself down doing good works to deserve to be saved and go to heaven. We are justified by faith in Christ and what He has done for us on the cross. It means being obedient to what the Lord has already shown you to do in your everyday life, as taught in Scripture. Also, listening for His voice and obeying His assignments to you personally. It is a huge challenge that only can be manifested in us by the Holy Spirit as we resolve to daily identify with Christ and give up the right to rule over Self. This is a goal we strive for as we go through our time on this earth.

Remember that the gift of Today is what you have been given. Yesterday is gone, and you can't open the door to the Future. Therefore, the application of His Word in obedience and trust is your assignment. With the Holy Spirit indwelling you, throw off any chains that have bound you and go forward in the freedom God has provided for you as you grow in Christ and look forward to His return.

Using the illustration of the *Today, No Knobs, Letting Go* painting and the principles that it represents has made it easier for me to remove the clutter from my life and take each day as it comes. I no longer feel the constant anxiety, worry, stress, and pressure that previously dominated me daily. It is my prayer that applying these things to your life will be as freeing to you as it is for me. It takes daily practice and cooperation with our Lord.

As evening begins to fade into night, release any lingering balloons with prayer and music notes of praise and thanksgiving. The Future is prepared for your next page of Today.

The next two sections of this book are designed for you to write your own personal journal. The first section is divided into pages for you to write your thoughts and prayers related to each chapter of this book. The second section is for your entries for each of your new Todays as you begin your own journey.

"May God himself, the God of peace, sanctify you through and through. May your whole spirit, soul and body be kept blameless at the coming of our Lord Jesus Christ. The one who calls you is faithful and he will do it" (1 Thessalonians 5:23–24).

Pages of Days Journal

The Painting

Date_____

_____

_____

_____

_____

_____

_____

_____

_____

_____

_____

_____

_____

_____

_____

_____

_____

_____

_____

_____

_____

_____

_____

_____

Realization

Date_____

_____

_____

_____

_____

_____

_____

_____

_____

_____

_____

_____

_____

_____

_____

_____

_____

_____

_____

_____

_____

_____

_____

_____

God's Instruction

Date_____

_____

_____

_____

_____

_____

_____

_____

_____

_____

_____

_____

_____

_____

_____

_____

_____

_____

_____

_____

_____

_____

_____

Today   Date_____

_____

_____

_____

_____

_____

_____

_____

_____

_____

_____

_____

_____

_____

_____

_____

_____

_____

_____

_____

_____

_____

_____

_____

Recognize the Enemy

Date_____

No Knobs, Past/Yesterday

Date_____

_____

_____

_____

_____

_____

_____

_____

_____

_____

_____

_____

_____

_____

_____

_____

_____

_____

_____

_____

_____

_____

_____

Longing

Date_____

_____

_____

_____

_____

_____

_____

_____

_____

_____

_____

_____

_____

_____

_____

_____

_____

_____

_____

_____

_____

_____

_____

Regrets

Date_____

_____

_____

_____

_____

_____

_____

_____

_____

_____

_____

_____

_____

_____

_____

_____

_____

_____

_____

_____

_____

_____

_____

_____

Decisions

Date_____

_____

_____

_____

_____

_____

_____

_____

_____

_____

_____

_____

_____

_____

_____

_____

_____

_____

_____

_____

_____

_____

Grief

Date_____

_____
_____
_____
_____
_____
_____
_____
_____
_____
_____
_____
_____
_____
_____
_____
_____
_____
_____
_____
_____
_____
_____
_____

No Knobs, Future/Tomorrow

Date_____

_____

_____

_____

_____

_____

_____

_____

_____

_____

_____

_____

_____

_____

_____

_____

_____

_____

_____

_____

_____

_____

_____

_____

In Christ Jesus

Date_____

Letting Go

Date_____

_____

_____

_____

_____

_____

_____

_____

_____

_____

_____

_____

_____

_____

_____

_____

_____

_____

_____

_____

_____

_____

_____

Surrender

Date_____

_____

_____

_____

_____

_____

_____

_____

_____

_____

_____

_____

_____

_____

_____

_____

_____

_____

_____

_____

_____

_____

Deception

Date_____

_____

_____

_____

_____

_____

_____

_____

_____

_____

_____

_____

_____

_____

_____

_____

_____

_____

_____

_____

_____

_____

_____

_____

Cross in the Tiles

Date_____

_____

_____

_____

_____

_____

_____

_____

_____

_____

_____

_____

_____

_____

_____

_____

_____

_____

_____

_____

_____

_____

_____

_____

_____

_____

_____

_____

Abiding in Christ

Date_____

Music Notes

Date_____

_____

_____

_____

_____

_____

_____

_____

_____

_____

_____

_____

_____

_____

_____

_____

_____

_____

_____

_____

_____

_____

_____

Gratitude

Date_____

_____

_____

_____

_____

_____

_____

_____

_____

_____

_____

_____

_____

_____

_____

_____

_____

_____

_____

_____

_____

_____

Evening and Morning

Date_____

_____

_____

_____

_____

_____

_____

_____

_____

_____

_____

_____

_____

_____

_____

_____

_____

_____

_____

_____

_____

_____

_____

_____

Pages of Days

Date_____

More Pages Of Days

Date_____

Date_____

_____
_____
_____
_____
_____
_____
_____
_____
_____
_____
_____
_____
_____
_____
_____
_____
_____
_____
_____
_____
_____
_____

Date_____

_____
_____
_____
_____
_____
_____
_____
_____
_____
_____
_____
_____
_____
_____
_____
_____
_____
_____
_____
_____
_____

Date_____

_____

_____

_____

_____

_____

_____

_____

_____

_____

_____

_____

_____

_____

_____

_____

_____

_____

_____

_____

_____

_____

_____

_____

Date_____

_____

_____

_____

_____

_____

_____

_____

_____

_____

_____

_____

_____

_____

_____

_____

_____

_____

_____

_____

_____

_____

_____

_____

_____

Date_____

Date_____

Date_____

_____

_____

_____

_____

_____

_____

_____

_____

_____

_____

_____

_____

_____

_____

_____

_____

_____

_____

_____

_____

_____

_____

_____

Date_____

Date_____

Date_____

_____

_____

_____

_____

_____

_____

_____

_____

_____

_____

_____

_____

_____

_____

_____

_____

_____

_____

_____

_____

_____

_____

_____

_____

_____

Date_____

_____

_____

_____

_____

_____

_____

_____

_____

_____

_____

_____

_____

_____

_____

_____

_____

_____

_____

_____

_____

_____

_____

_____

_____

Date_____

Date_____

Date_____

_____

_____

_____

_____

_____

_____

_____

_____

_____

_____

_____

_____

_____

_____

_____

_____

_____

_____

_____

_____

_____

_____

Date_____

_____

_____

_____

_____

_____

_____

_____

_____

_____

_____

_____

_____

_____

_____

_____

_____

_____

_____

_____

_____

_____

_____

Date_____

_____

_____

_____

_____

_____

_____

_____

_____

_____

_____

_____

_____

_____

_____

_____

_____

_____

_____

_____

_____

_____

_____

Date_____

_____

_____

_____

_____

_____

_____

_____

_____

_____

_____

_____

_____

_____

_____

_____

_____

_____

_____

_____

_____

_____

_____

_____

Date_____

_____

_____

_____

_____

_____

_____

_____

_____

_____

_____

_____

_____

_____

_____

_____

_____

_____

_____

_____

_____

_____

_____

_____

_____

Date_____

_____

_____

_____

_____

_____

_____

_____

_____

_____

_____

_____

_____

_____

_____

_____

_____

_____

_____

_____

_____

_____

_____

_____

Date_____

Date_____

_____

_____

_____

_____

_____

_____

_____

_____

_____

_____

_____

_____

_____

_____

_____

_____

_____

_____

_____

_____

_____

_____

_____

Date_____

_____

_____

_____

_____

_____

_____

_____

_____

_____

_____

_____

_____

_____

_____

_____

_____

_____

_____

_____

_____

_____

_____

_____

Date_____

Date_____

_____

_____

_____

_____

_____

_____

_____

_____

_____

_____

_____

_____

_____

_____

_____

_____

_____

_____

_____

_____

_____

_____

_____

Date_____

_____

_____

_____

_____

_____

_____

_____

_____

_____

_____

_____

_____

_____

_____

_____

_____

_____

_____

_____

_____

_____

_____

Date_____

Date_____

_____

_____

_____

_____

_____

_____

_____

_____

_____

_____

_____

_____

_____

_____

_____

_____

_____

_____

_____

_____

_____

_____

Date_____

_____

_____

_____

_____

_____

_____

_____

_____

_____

_____

_____

_____

_____

_____

_____

_____

_____

_____

_____

_____

_____

_____

Date_____

_____

_____

_____

_____

_____

_____

_____

_____

_____

_____

_____

_____

_____

_____

_____

_____

_____

_____

_____

_____

_____

_____

CPSIA information can be obtained
at www.ICGtesting.com
Printed in the USA
LVHW031458140223
739479LV00015B/1307